KENTUCKY

Here is the story of the land and of the people of a beautiful and fertile state that slopes away from Big Black Mountain to the Mississippi.

Here is a land where blue grass grows lush on a bed of limestone over half a billion years old, once the floor of an ancient sea. This is a state where geologic forces carved the Mammoth Caves, charted for 150 miles. Fossil boneyards tell of prehistoric life.

Indians hunted on this land, French and British claimed it. Harrod and Boone settled it and a flood of pioneers poured through Cumberland Gap to face hardships and Indians and to carve a state from the wilderness. Here is Kentucky today, its land, people, horses, industries, farms, arts, lakes, rivers and its enchantment.

The preservation of areas of historic significance and the many state parks speak of the pride of Kentuckians in the past as they look toward a modern and prosperous future.

Enchantment of America

KENTUCKY

By Allan Carpenter

Illustrations by Darrell Wiskur

CHILDRENS PRESS, CHICAGO

Consultants
Joseph R. Schwendeman, University of Kentucky, Lexington
Martha Ellison, Coordinator of Curriculum Development,
State Department of Education

For their advice, counsel and gracious help, the author thanks:
Edward T. Breathitt, Governor
J. R. Schwendeman, Chairman, Department of Geography and
　　Professor of Geography, University of Kentucky, Lexington
Martha Ellison, Coordinator of Curriculum Development,
　　State Department of Education
J. O. Matlick, Commissioner of Natural Resources, Frankfort
Kentucky Department of Commerce
Tom Balow
Public Library, Evanston, Illinois

Library of Congress Catalog Card Number: 67-20094

Contents

A True Story to Set the Scene

"We Will Sing One Song"

Somewhere, sometime (probably in 1852) a young man sat down to compose a song, and in doing so created an intriguing minor mystery that adds to the enchantment of Kentucky. Most important, by his act he tied the whole world to Kentucky with bonds of sentiment that probably never will be broken.

The composer was America's master of song, Stephen Collins Foster. The mystery is simply that no one knows where he was when he wrote the song. Some experts even doubt that he ever set foot in Kentucky. In view of the vast information known about Stephen Foster, it seems even more a mystery why there are no exact records about the song that has become known the world around as *My Old Kentucky Home*.

Stephen Foster's father had a cousin, former United States Senator, Judge John Rowan, who owned a summer home called Federal Hill near Bardstown. Today the beautiful and stately home and grounds, purchased for $65,000 and given to Kentucky in 1922 by public subscription, are maintained as My Old Kentucky Home Shrine and State Park. Mrs. Joseph M. Wycoff, Curator of the park, is positive that Foster sat at the fine old desk in the mansion, surrounded by the sights and sounds of a typical Kentucky plantation.

She is sure that in this setting he wrote of the sun shining brightly,

and of the corn tops ripening while the birds made music all the day. He mused about the brave Negro families who sang and did their work even though their lives placed a "shadow on the heart" and they feared that hard times would come knocking at the door of the slave house. It is this slave house that is really the "home" in the song.

All this could be true, but unfortunately, there are no records to verify it.

It seems almost certain, however, that Stephen Foster visited Federal Hill, probably more than once. Undoubtedly he had been struck by the home life of both the aristocratic owners and their slaves, who are said to have been "well treated." Stephen's visits appear to be verified by his brother Morrison, who wrote in his own handwriting "He (Stephen) was not a protegé of Judge Rowan but only an occasional visitor at Federal Hill."

Stephen Foster lived in Cincinnati from 1846 to 1850. From here it would have been easy for him to visit Federal Hill during that period. Other members of his family are known to have gone there at various times. Judge Rowan died in 1843, but his son John was the master of Federal Hill after his father's death.

Composer Will S. Hays wrote in 1893, "When or under what circumstances the famous song was written few, if any but the author, ever knew, but it is supposed . . . that Foster evidently meant Judge Rowan's residence, known as 'Federal Hill,' for it was really the only 'Old Kentucky Home' that Foster ever had, and he loved it."

Foster expert Evelyn Foster Morneweck states that "All the testimony seems to point to the fact that Stephen undoubtedly was an occasional guest of the Rowans at 'Federal Hill.' "

"In this idyllic spot," wrote Raymond Walters, "Stephen obtained his love for Kentucky. . . . Wherever *My Old Kentucky Home* was written, Kentucky has every sentimental right to its official song."

The exact facts are really not important except to add the spice of mystery to the story. What does matter is that America's tragic troubadour has been able to express the feeling for a place and bring out the deep emotions of its people. In this song he has made Kentucky the symbol of home around the world, representing the longing for home of human beings everywhere.

Lay of the Land

"Second Paradise"

Kentucky is a "second paradise" rhapsodized Daniel Boone. A Methodist minister put the same feeling in another way when he wrote "Heaven is a Kentucky of a place!" An early English tourist declared, "Kentucky . . . is extending in every direction over a tract of the finest and most fertile country in the world; and it is from . . . this vast country that America will derive her future greatness and establish new empires. . . ." What was there about this land and its location that inspired such extravagant comment?

The average person would probably divide Kentucky into three very distinct regions—Eastern Mountain, Bluegrass, and Western. To the geographer there are six regions—Jackson Purchase in the west, the Western Coal Field, the Knobs, the Bluegrass, and finally the Eastern Mountains region (sometimes called the Eastern Coal Field), nestled against the western slopes of the Appalachians. The Knobs region is a strangely shaped narrow area making a crescent around the southern half of the Bluegrass region. The Knobs area has been called "one of the most distinctive regions of the world." The Bluegrass area is divided into an Outer Bluegrass and an Inner Bluegrass, roughly in the center of the Outer.

The five major physiographic regions are somewhat similar—the Eastern Coal Field or Cumberland Plateau, the Bluegrass, the Mississippian Plateau, the Western Coal Field, and the Jackson Purchase. The Knobs and Inner Bluegrass are considered as "sub-regions."

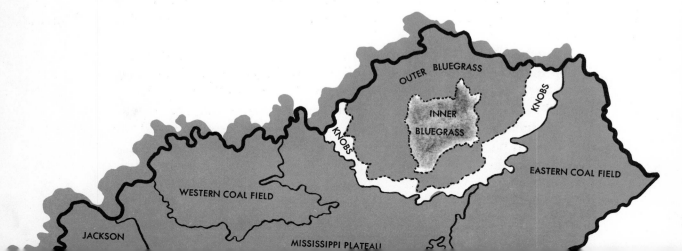

Kentucky is bordered by seven states—Virginia, West Virginia, Ohio, Indiana, Illinois, Missouri and Tennessee; only two states have more neighbors than Kentucky. There is a tradition that part of the boundary with West Virginia was chosen by mistake. The boundary commissioners decided that the boundary would be placed on the larger fork of the Big Sandy River. During the night the Tug Fork was swollen with rain, and the commissioners quickly proclaimed this to be the boundary. They did not wait to see that when the flood waters went down the Levisa Fork was actually larger. This action added a sizeable area of rich land to Kentucky.

Kentucky covers an area of 40,395 square miles, making it the 37th state in size. From a high point of 4,150 feet at Big Black Mountain, the state slopes away to its lowest point on the Mississippi River.

A Well-Watered Land

The Mississippi makes a western border for Kentucky for 69 miles, and provides the state with one of the strangest twists of geography in the country. The far southwestern tip of Kentucky is formed by the Mississippi turning in almost a complete circle. Inside the loop of river the circle of land, which belongs to Kentucky, cannot be reached from the rest of the state without crossing either Tennessee or Missouri. It cannot be reached at all by land except from a narrow tongue of soil stretching up from Tennessee.

One of the nation's longest river borders is formed by the turns and twists of the majestic and beautiful Ohio River which gives Kentucky a 680-mile long shoreline; in the same area on the north, the Ohio bounds three different states.

Altogether, Kentucky has over 13,000 miles of streams and rivers. Other major rivers are the 238-mile Kentucky River, winding from the eastern mountains through the fertile Bluegrass to the Ohio River; the 370-mile Green River, also emptying into the Ohio; the Cumberland River, which begins and ends its 687-mile course in Kentucky, and the downstream portion of the mighty Tennessee River.

Among many other rivers are the Tradewater River, Licking River and the Kentucky-West Virginia boundary river—the Big Sandy. Some-

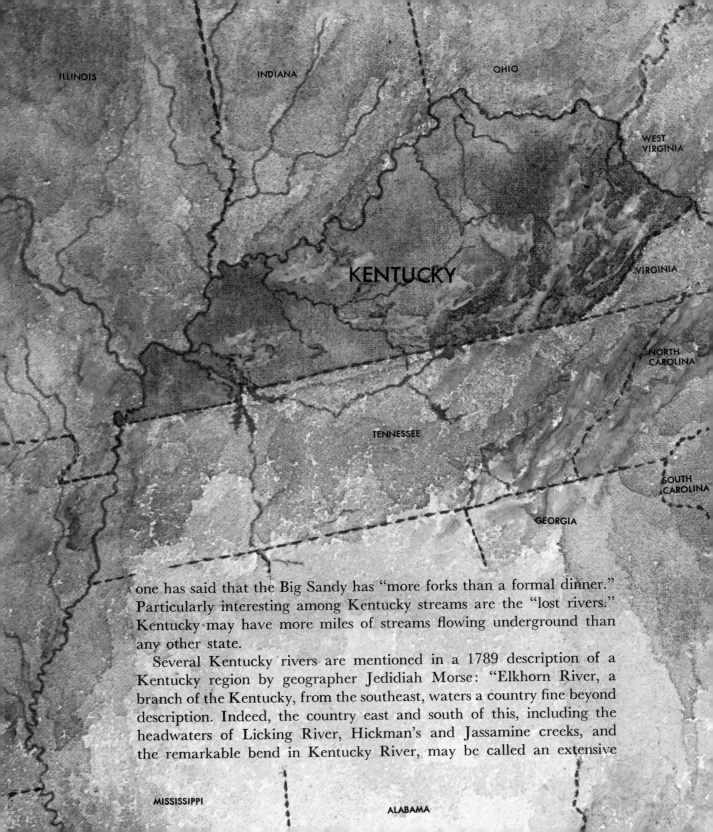

ILLINOIS

INDIANA

OHIO

WEST VIRGINIA

KENTUCKY

VIRGINIA

NORTH CAROLINA

TENNESSEE

SOUTH CAROLINA

GEORGIA

MISSISSIPPI

ALABAMA

one has said that the Big Sandy has "more forks than a formal dinner."
Particularly interesting among Kentucky streams are the "lost rivers."
Kentucky may have more miles of streams flowing underground than
any other state.

Several Kentucky rivers are mentioned in a 1789 description of a
Kentucky region by geographer Jedidiah Morse: "Elkhorn River, a
branch of the Kentucky, from the southeast, waters a country fine beyond
description. Indeed, the country east and south of this, including the
headwaters of Licking River, Hickman's and Jassamine creeks, and
the remarkable bend in Kentucky River, may be called an extensive

garden. . . . The banks, or rather precipices, of the Kentucky and Dick's (Dix) Rivers are to be reckoned among the natural curiosities of this country. Here the astonished eye beholds 300 or 400 feet of solid perpendicular rocks—in some parts of the limestone kind and in others of fine white marble. . . . These rivers have the appearance of deep artificial canals. . . ."

14

Lakes—From Earthquake to Bulldozer

The largest bodies of water in Kentucky are man-made, forming eleven major artificial lakes or "impoundments" in the state. Lake Cumberland, covering 50,250 acres, is the biggest lake entirely within the state. The 2,380-mile shoreline of Kentucky Lake is said to be the longest of any artificial lake in the world. However, it is shared with Tennessee, although the largest part is in Kentucky. The lake covers much of the course of the Tennessee River in Kentucky.

Mammoth Lake Barkley, completed in 1965, is a kind of twin of Kentucky Lake, covering much of the lower reaches of the Cumberland River and also extending into Tennessee. Rough River Reservoir, Dale Hollow Reservoir, and Nolin Reservoir are other large Kentucky bodies of water. In the period since 1950, 41 state-owned lakes of varying sizes have been created in Kentucky. Among the smaller natural lakes of the state, some of the most interesting are the strangely shaped "oxbow" lakes, formed mostly when the Ohio or Mississippi abandoned an old channel and left bodies of water curved like oxbows.

One of the world's strangest lakes is Reelfoot, formed by an earthquake in 1811. Waters of the Mississippi poured into this region which had been lowered by the quake. Most of Reelfoot is in Tennessee, however.

Altogether, the water surface of Kentucky covers 532 square miles.

In Ancient Days

Kentucky has been in the making for hundreds of millions of years. The story told in the rocks of the state is one of ages of glacier melting, mountain rising, sea-draining, cave cutting, coal laying, and coral growing.

Much that is world-famous about Kentucky can be traced to the incredible forces of the great geologic drama. The carpet of bluegrass grows lush on the bed of limestone over half a billion years old which was once the bottom of an extensive shallow sea. Coal mines in the Appalachians reveal the secrets of mountains older than the Alps, pressing together layers of plant life that once made a swampland on the

15

edge of an area teeming with small life. Visitors to Mammoth Cave view Nature still at work as she was millions of years ago, sculpting limestone in a giant underground workshop.

The huge cave region of Kentucky, in fact, is said to be "unique among all the regions of the world." There are over 2,000 caves in Kentucky—more than in any other state—where water has eaten away limestone and other water-soluble minerals, leaving among other remains a "land of 10,000 sinks"—eroded holes.

More than 230 million years ago the Appalachian Mountains began a slow rising which brought them to great heights over the ages. Then during the eons they began to wear away, succumbing to the tireless effects of wind and water. The Cumberland and Pine mountain ranges are the remains of a great westerly-sloping plateau. These mountains are formed mostly by erosion, with the cutting away of the plateau by streams and wind into a region of narrow valleys between sharp ridges.

The Knobs region takes its name from the knob-like shapes of the remnants of the eroded plateaus which border the mountain region.

In Shelby County there are even the remains of what was almost a volcano—called a crypto-volcano—one that didn't quite happen to go off—very unusual for this region of the earth. This strange mound of earth with its obvious volcano-like shape can be spotted from U.S. Highway 60.

Kentucky is one of the richest areas of the world for fossils. It has been called the "nation's outstanding prehistoric boneyard." One of the greatest fossil areas anywhere was found at Big Bone Lick in 1729 by French-Canadian explorer Charles de Longueil. The salt springs that had attracted the ancient animals in such great numbers were still running. Many of the lumbering creatures became stuck in the soft mud or quicksand of the region and left their remains for the marvel of future ages.

When the party of James Douglas explored the region in 1773 they made tent poles of the mastodon ribs and sat on benches fashioned from the vertebrae. When they left, the Douglas party carried with them 10-pound teeth, tusks 10 and 11 feet long and "soup" bones five-feet long.

Later, from this same Big Bone Lick, Thomas Jefferson assembled one of the finest fossil collections ever gathered, but this ended in great tragedy for the scientific world of all ages. A servant, ignorant of the invaluable collection's real purpose, had the bones all ground up for fertilizer.

Fossils have been found in many other parts of the state. They range from the most insignificant sea creatures of the earliest periods to enormous mammoths, mastodons, and moose, elk, beaver, and wolves of giant size.

Climate

The climate of Kentucky is milder than in many states of the same latitude. The temperate winters average 40° in the south for about the coldest six-week period and light snows stay on the ground only a short time. Summers are moderate, and in the higher regions summer evenings are almost always cool. The sun shines for more than half the possible time. Precipitation averages 41.32 inches. The growing season ranges from 210 days in the extreme southwest to 180 days in the northeast and mountain areas.

Collecting Your Thoughts

The kind of a land people live in has an effect on their lives. List as many things as you can about the land of Kentucky, both past and present, that have had an influence on the people of the state.

17

Footsteps on the Land

The Ancient Ones

The body was laid to rest carefully on a ledge. She was a tall (5 feet, 10 inches) person, apparently of an aristocratic family who had died of a stab wound about the time Christ was born. In 1812, miners working in Mammoth Cave found her body on what came to be known as Mummy Ledge. Tradition says that her rich clothing was woven of basswood fibers, covered by a robe of deerskin with patterns painted in formal decorations. As with most women she must have been a lover of hats, for seven picturesque headdresses (one for each day of the week) lay beside her body. Her necklace was made of small beads and evil-looking bear claws. Near her hand lay a small flute-like musical instrument.

Unfortunately, this valuable relic of the past has disappeared. However, many traces of the ancient peoples who once lived in what is now Kentucky have been preserved down to the present day in every county of the state.

Hundreds of prehistoric mounds dot Kentucky. Some of these were raised by the oldest peoples of the state. Other mounds were heaped up by the historic Indians. Some of them contain only the trash tossed out of kitchens, while others may contain burial remains or may cover whole villages. At least one group of prehistoric people of Kentucky periodically burnt their towns, covered them with a mound of dirt and built a new town on the top.

One of the most unusual mounds is that near Quicksand; it consists of a huge pile of stones, brought from a considerable distance. Among the most visited mounds are the six still found in Central Park at Ashland. The five-mile-long artificial canal near Cayce was one of the most unusual works of the mound builders. This is thought to have connected two prehistoric cities.

The remains found in a prehistoric burial ground at Wickliffe have been uncovered carefully. There visitors may see 153 skeletons in the exact positions given them in burial. Prehistoric fortifications, such as those near Berea, also are found in various parts of the state.

Mysterious containers were found near Flemingsburg. These are as much as 6 feet across and carved into the sandstone for 9 to 12 inches. These are known as Indian Kettles. Nearby are circular sandstone pieces as large as the kettles, which appear to be their covers.

Hollows have been found carved into sandstone rocks in which hominy was pounded. One of these hominy hollows, discovered near Munfordville, weighed two tons. It is thought that some of these prehistoric people were advanced enough to use mechanical means to grind their hominy. Near Madisonville was discovered a series of large hominy holes reminiscent of a small factory. Some experts believe that the prehistoric technicians devised a series of mechanical pestles that pounded the corn in these holes. The power source they used is not known.

"Land of Tomorrow"

In early historical times the Indian population of what is now Kentucky was never very large. Much of the present state seems to have been agreed upon as a kind of intertribal park, where many tribes enjoyed the rights of hunting and fishing in the pleasant region which they called "Land of Tomorrow." There were few permanent Indian settlements there during this period.

The Indian name for Kentucky was an Iroquois term *Ken-ta-ke,* meaning "place of old fields." The word "old" apparently should be translated "admired" or "revered."

Then in the early 1600's the fierce Iroquois Indians were able to obtain guns from the Dutch settlers of New York and begin to drive the other tribes from their lands. As early as 1645 groups of Indians were fleeing across Kentucky, pursued by the Iroquois. By 1690 present Kentucky was almost completely cleared of its Indian population.

Later a few straggling Indian bands returned to make their homes. A group of Shawnee settled a village in southeastern Clark County which they called Eskippakithiki. This was occupied from about 1718 to 1754. Lower Shawneetown was begun by groups of Shawnee, Delaware, and Mingo Indians around 1729 but was abandoned before the French and Indian War. These were probably the last Indian settlements in what is now Kentucky.

First Stirrings

The French claimed all the vast regions west of the Appalachian Mountains to the "Western Sea," and it is probable that French adventurers visited present Kentucky. However, the first record of a European visit to the region was that of English Colonel Abram Wood of Virginia in 1654.

In the decades that followed there may have been occasional European visitors. John Peter Salley reached the Ohio River but was captured by the French. Pierre Joseph Celeron, le Sieur de Bienville, made a strange expedition down the Ohio River, planting lead plates to claim the land for the King of France. In 1750 he passed much of what is now the Kentucky shore on his way.

The British did not recognize the French claims to the region, and in order to press their own claims they encouraged exploration. The Loyal Land Company of Virginia was organized and gained a grant of 800,000 acres across the mountains. They sent a party led by Dr. Thomas Walker and they explored this region for several weeks in 1750 before returning to Virginia.

In 1751 the noted Christopher Gist made one of the first extensive explorations of the Ohio River country. He visited Big Bone Lick and also intended to stop at the Falls of the Ohio (present Louisville), but friendly Shawnee warned him that hostile Indians were camped there. He then made his way over the mountains and into North Carolina. Gist noted in his journal that he had visited a group of French traders who had made a kind of settlement among the Indians at Lower Shawneetown. This must be considered the first European settlement in present Kentucky, but it was not permanent.

An intriguing quotation by Colonel George Croghan tells of the fate of this settlement: "On the Ohio, just below the mouth of the Scioto, on a high bank near forty feet, formerly stood the Shawneese town called Lower Town—which was all carried away, except three or four houses, by a great flood. I was in the town at the time. Although the banks of the Ohio were so high, yet the water was nine feet over the top, which obliged the whole town to take to their canoes and move with their effects to the hills. They returned to the south bank of the Ohio, but abandoned the settlement because of fear of the Virginians during the French and Indian War."

When that war was over, the French had been driven from the continent, and the British were masters of the region from the Atlantic to the Mississippi. However, King George III issued his proclamation of 1763 which prohibited settlers from moving over the western slope of the Appalachians. Many were bitterly disappointed over this order.

Nevertheless, hunters and others continued to travel the forbidden land.

A Boone for the West

One of these travelers became known (at least in legend) as the man who opened the American frontier. Daniel Boone previously had been exploring much of the east coast, including Florida. He heard the stories of John Findley who had been one of the "Long Hunters" in Kentucky. They were given this name because of the long periods they spent hunting in the wilderness. In 1769, Findley took Boone over an easy pass in the mountains where present-day Tennessee, Kentucky and Virginia meet. This has come to be called Cumberland Gap, and can be viewed from a scenic lookout in the magnificent national park created in this historic area. Two years later Daniel Boone, according to his own account, "returned to my family, being determined to reside in Kentucky which I esteemed a second paradise."

Meanwhile, James Harrod also had been exploring in Kentucky and he led a group of 31 settlers to a place he called Harrodstown (now Harrodsburg) which they founded in 1774, making it the oldest permanent European settlement in what is now Kentucky.

About this time Colonel Richard Henderson and the Hart brothers, Nathaniel, Thomas and David, were encouraged by Daniel Boone to form a huge company to settle in Kentucky. At a solemn council, the Cherokee Indians were paid a large sum for land in Kentucky, although both the governors of North Carolina and Virginia were against the plan. The new business was first named for Henderson and later was called the Transylvania Company. This company hired Boone to help get the first colony started. He blazed a trail, later known as Boone's

Trace, and on a terrace of the Kentucky River on April 5, 1775, Boone and a party of 30 men began to build Fort Boonesborough. When Colonel Henderson arrived he called the settlers together to make plans for a simple kind of government. Before these discussions began under the branches of a tremendous old elm, the settlers heard Squire Boone, Daniel's brother, preach the first sermon in present Kentucky. Later under the same benevolent old tree, Squire Boone performed the first marriage ceremony in Kentucky.

As soon as the rude cabins and quickly-built furniture were ready, the settlers sent for their wives and families, who arrived in September. The women immediately began the task of preserving and storing supplies for the coming winter. They were also busy spinning, and weaving and turning fats into soap and candles. Newcomers to the settlement included George Rogers Clark, whose name was to become well known a little later.

BOONESBOROUGH

Scalps for George III

By this time, the fighting of the Revolutionary War already had begun on the East Coast, and the infant colony of Kentucky was to play a part in that struggle.

The British did as much as they could to stir up the Indians against the colonists, especially in the West. On July 14, 1776, only 10 days after the Declaration of Independence was signed, a hostile Indian party reached Boonesborough. They took captive Daniel Boone's daughter and two daughters of a Colonel Calloway. As the Indians fled with their captives toward the Indian villages in Ohio, Elizabeth Calloway broke bits of brush and twigs and even managed to tear off pieces of her clothing to leave a trail for rescuers. She also dug her heels into the earth as hard as she could to leave a trail.

A rescue party of nine men led by Boone and Colonel John Floyd set out, following the marks left by Elizabeth. With them were the fiancés of the captured girls. When the rescuers caught up, the Indians left their captives unharmed and fled without a fight.

In December, 1776, the legislature of Virginia organized the region as Kentucky County, a county of Virginia. This was the first official use of Kentucky as a name for the area. The people of Harrodsburg had sent George Rogers Clark and John G. Jones with a petition for this, and so Harrodsburg was named as the county seat.

Virginia refused to recognize Colonel Henderson's claim to the lands for which he had paid the Indians 10,000 pounds, but later, they gave him a grant of 200,000 acres in the present-day county that bears his name.

In 1777 George Rogers Clark made his plans to drive the British from what was then the West. By this time, enough people had arrived in Kentucky so that he could recruit his small army there, as he was authorized to do by Governor Patrick Henry of Virginia. The heroic exploits of Clark and his Kentucky riflemen are famed in the stories of war, as they captured Illinois, crawled through the winter slush to capture Vincennes, Indiana, and finally made sure that the West would remain in American hands.

Daniel Boone and 15 other men were captured by a Shawnee party early in 1778. The braves ordered Boone to lead them to Boonesborough, but he finally persuaded them to wait until spring. He knew how weak the settlement was. Boone was able to escape from his captors in June and hurried back to warn of the attack. He found that he had been given up for dead, and his wife had gone back to their former home.

The fort was quickly strengthened just before 400 Indians and 40 Canadians attacked. There were only about 60 defenders, but they stood off the Indians almost miraculously for 10 days and finally drove them away. Another heroic defense against heavy odds was made by the people of Logan's Fort under Colonel Benjamin Logan. Yet another brave defense was successful at McAfee in 1779.

In August, 1782, a force of almost 1,000 Indians under British Captain William Caldwell and Simon Girty attacked Bryan Station, confident they would have an easy victory. With the help of the women and even the children, the station held out bravely until reinforcements could reach the scene. Fearing more reinforcements, Caldwell retreated toward the Ohio River. Some authorities claim that this was the battle which finally halted the British invasion of Kentucky.

The defenders of Bryan Station, under Colonel John Todd, followed the retreating enemy. When they caught up with the large British force, Daniel Boone advised them to wait for more reinforcements, but they disregarded his counsel, attacked at once and suffered a severe loss; 60 of their force of 176 were killed and 7 were made prisoners. Israel Boone, son of Daniel, was among those killed in the savage "Battle of Blue Licks," lasting only about 15 minutes. His father escaped in his usual pattern of daring and luck by swimming across the river under water.

The victory was useless for the British, however, because by this time the settlers were aroused and were hurrying from every direction to attack the British force, which soon fled back across the Ohio River. The Revolutionary War was over in Kentucky.

Unfortunately, the Indian attacks kept up for several more years. One of the worst of these came in the fall of 1786. Members of the McNitt Company camped along the banks of the Little Laurel River. Rejoicing at reaching the Kentucky territory, they relaxed and failed to post a guard. The tragic error resulted in 24 settlers being slain by a band of Indians. A party from Crab Orchard discovered the bodies, buried them high on the banks of the river and named the place "Defeated Camp."

The Commonwealth of Kentucky

In spite of the dangers of Indians and the trail, however, a flood of pioneers from the East surged through the Cumberland Gap, breaking the barrier of the Alleghenies. Between 1775 and 1795 more than 100,000 people made their way over the Gap. In one year, alone, more than 20,000 people passed over the Wilderness Road. This was the first of the vast movement of people who would someday populate the American West.

Danville was made the seat of Virginia's government in the West. After the formation of the country under the Articles of Confederation, increasing talk was heard favoring admission of Kentucky as a separate state of the Confederation. A long period of quarreling began. Some people felt that the region should remain a part of Virginia. Others argued that it should become an entirely separate country, while some even wanted it to become a part of the Spanish domain then west of the Mississippi. A total of ten different conventions met to determine the future of the region. Finally a constitution was drafted at Danville in April, 1792, and adopted. On June 1, 1792, the Commonwealth of Kentucky was admitted to the Union as the 15th state. It was the first state to be carved out of the vast territories west of the original 13 colonies, the forerunner of others which someday would make the United States a great nation spread from coast to coast.

Frankfort was chosen as capital of the commonwealth and General Isaac Shelby was the first governor.

Collecting Your Thoughts

If you could visit any one of the early settlements of Kentucky from the prehistoric period to statehood, which would you choose?

Yesterday and Today

Progress and Disagreement

The early period of statehood was one of change, growth, progress and dissension. By 1793 the danger of Indian attack had almost vanished. Kentuckians became interested in what was known as the French-Genêt conspiracy and many helped Edmund Genêt in his activities. The people were divided over such problems as the rights of the states as opposed to the new Federal Constitution and how to guarantee the rights of the individual under both the state and federal governments.

A bear was responsible for bringing to light Kentucky's most astounding natural wonder. A hunter named Houchins was tracking the wounded animal in 1799 when he discovered one of the world's marvels. That same year a land grant was recorded for the region described as "200 acres of second-rate land lying on the Green River," and including "two petre caves"—not even named.

It is interesting to note that the saltpetre, or niter, in the cave soil was useful in making gunpowder during the War of 1812. Today the Mammoth Cave area is no longer described as "second rate."

One of the most sensational court cases in American history occurred in Kentucky. The mysterious and mistrusted former Vice President of the United States, Aaron Burr, was thought to be plotting to create an independent country west of the Mississippi. Twice he was brought to trial before the Federal Court of the Kentucky District but each time he was found innocent of treason charges.

Even more "earthshaking" were two events of 1811—one natural, the other man-made. An earthquake vibrated much of the continent, but was centered in the region of New Madrid, Missouri, just opposite Kentucky. The first terrible shake lasted four minutes. There was thunder and lightning, and one Louisville account spoke of "complete darkness and saturation of the atmosphere with sulphuric vapor." Eighty-seven separate shocks were felt in a single week after the first quake. The quakes continued through most of 1812. An interesting comment on all of this appeared in a Pennsylvania newspaper, which reported that Louisvillians, in paroxysms of piety, raised large sums of money for a church during the quakes, but ended up spending it on a theater when the quakes were definitely ended.

The other significant event of 1811 was the arrival of the *New Orleans,* the first steamboat. Puffing along the Ohio and Mississippi, it heralded the beginning of a great age of riverboating when the rivers would be supreme in the life of the state.

Many from Kentucky took part in the War of 1812. The 5,500 Kentuckians who fought in the Battle of New Orleans made up a large part of the American troops in the battle. They played a major role in the great victory of General Andrew Jackson there in 1814.

Four years later, in 1818, General Jackson and Governor Isaac Shelby negotiated with the Chickasaw for a wilderness region west of the Tennessee River. The government paid $300,000 for the 8,500 square miles of territory, which became known as the Jackson Purchase.

During much of this period the history of Kentucky was concerned greatly with developments in transportation, mining, commerce and industry, and agriculture, discussed in later sections.

As time went by, however, one of the greatest concerns was the growing problem of slavery. Slaves had been brought into the state almost from the beginning of its settlement. As early as 1799 ministers of religion were refused the right to hold office in Kentucky because it was felt they might vote some laws against slavery. However, conditions were not right in many parts of Kentucky for slaves to be used profitably. The large landholders of the Bluegrass region were the ones most concerned with holding on to slavery, but their numbers were relatively small.

In the less wealthy regions and in the cities where there were few slaves, people were against holding their fellow humans in bondage. Outside abolitionists (those who wanted to do away with slavery) sent their representatives into Kentucky to rouse the people against slavery. There were also many abolitionists within the state. General Cassius M. Clay, who was born in Madison County, became the publisher of the Lexington *True American* newspaper and fought slavery with great hatred.

In the election of 1860 two Kentucky-born candidates ran for the presidency of the United States. These were Abraham Lincoln and

John C. Breckinridge. However, neither man carried his native state in the election.

A House Divided

When war came in 1861, the people of Kentucky were bitterly divided. As a border state, Kentucky was drawn to both sides. Kentucky experienced the tragedy of father fighting against son, and brother against brother on a scale perhaps never equaled elsewhere. The family ties and way of life of many Kentucky people drew them to the South, but the people of Kentucky were said to have "an almost reverent feeling about the United States Constitution," which even further confused their loyalties.

A few examples will show the heart-rending situation. Of the two sons of Kentucky's senior United States Senator John J. Crittenden, one became a Union general, the other a general of the Confederate army. Lincoln's strongest backer in Kentucky was Robert J. Breckinridge of Lexington, but Breckinridge's two oldest sons fought with the South. Of the five grandsons of Henry Clay, three fought with the Confederacy and two with the Union. Much of the family of Mary Todd Lincoln, the President's Kentucky-born wife, fought with the Confederacy.

Strangest of all, the President of the United States, Abraham Lincoln, and the President of the United Confederate States, Jefferson Davis, were both natives of Kentucky—born less than 100 miles apart and within a year of each other.

In spite of all the dissension, the regular government of the state throughout the war refused to break the Union ties. Most experts agree that the majority of the people of Kentucky also sided with the Union. Nevertheless, a convention meeting in 1861 at Russellville proclaimed Kentucky to be the 13th state of the Confederacy. However, because of its position between the two warring regions, Kentucky tried to remain neutral, and both sides agreed to respect this neutrality.

In spite of this, Kentucky became the scene of fierce and continued fighting. Strategic Cumberland Gap changed hands four different times, and Lexington three times. Frankfort was the only loyal Union capital captured by the Confederates. It was later recaptured. Richmond was

the center of conflict throughout most of the war. Altogether 400 battles and skirmishes were fought in Kentucky during the war.

Kentucky neutrality was first broken by the Confederates, who seized the bluffs at Columbus and fortified them with heavy cannon. They stretched a huge chain a mile long across the Mississippi to keep Union boats from passing up and down the river. Each link in this chain weighed over 15 pounds. General Ulysses S. Grant tried to capture Columbus but found it was impregnable, and he almost suffered a great defeat. Later, by going around Columbus and winning the Battle of Shiloh, Grant was able to cut Columbus off and cause it to surrender.

Earlier, Grant had taken possession of Paducah, and the town was occupied for the rest of the war.

Late in 1861 Union troops planned to capture the Big Sandy River Valley to avoid any southern attack from Virginia which might sweep through the Ohio Valley. This campaign was under Colonel James A. Garfield. On January 10, 1862, Garfield led his troops to win the Battle of Middle Creek, near Prestonsburg. This was the first sizeable Union victory of the entire war and it brought Garfield a general's rank, starting him on the path to the presidency.

An account is given of how before this battle Garfield himself and one aide took a small boat down the flooded Big Sandy River to Catlettsburg to get much needed supplies. Garfield loaded the steamer *Sandy Valley* with the goods he needed, but the captain refused to pilot him back up river to his troops. According to the story, Garfield seized the wheel himself, and without knowing the river piloted the boat safely back.

In August, 1862, Confederate forces had their first victory in Kentucky at Richmond. Late in 1862 the Confederates used the biggest gun then known, "Long Tom," to capture Cumberland Gap for the first time. Confederate General Braxton Bragg continued the southern campaign in Kentucky by pushing into the interior of the state.

Suddenly, on October 8, 1862, Bragg's troops came upon units of Northern General Don Carlos Buell near Perryville; neither side was prepared for the battle which was fought—the bloodiest in Kentucky history. A total of 40,000 troops on both sides took part; Union forces lost 4,241 men, and the Confederates 3,396. Although neither side could

30

claim a victory, this has been called the deciding engagement of the war in Kentucky. General Bragg withdrew, and it became clear that no further Confederate military attempts to take Kentucky would succeed.

General Bragg was much criticized in the South for his handling of the Kentucky campaign, especially for his many unnecessary delays. Some experts feel that if he had marched as quickly as possible to the north he might have captured and held Louisville before Union troops could have stopped him. Such a firm Confederate hold on the heart of the Ohio River Valley might even have changed the course of the war completely.

There were other organized battles fought later in Kentucky, but for the most part the people suffered from guerrilla attacks. Notorious William Clark Quantrill, who had gained a fearsome reputation for his cruel and heartless raids in Missouri, moved his operations to Kentucky, and the people endured awful afflictions in this cruelest kind of warfare.

Even the most awful wars, however, have their lighter sides, and in Kentucky the war was said to be responsible for the creation of one of the state's favorite dishes. The story is told that on one of Confederate raider John Hunt Morgan's raids in Kentucky food supplies were so scarce that the French cook, Gus Jaubert, had only some blackbirds killed by the men. With these he prepared a highly seasoned thick soup, throwing in all the vegetables he could find. The result was delicious— the beginning of burgoo—a dish especially popular today at political campaigns and horse sales, and at the annual gatherings of the famous Kentucky Colonels.

A total of 90,000 soldiers from Kentucky served the Union cause during the war, and there were 45,000 from the state in Confederate service. Strangely there were more Confederate volunteers from Kentucky than there were from Virginia, and, equally odd, there were more drafted for the Union side in Kentucky than were drafted from Ohio.

A Modern State

Although Kentucky had remained loyal, after the war the state suffered almost as much during the reconstruction period as the states of

31

the deep South. Much of the market for Kentucky's produce and goods had been in the South, and this business almost came to a halt. One of the marvels of the postwar period was the imagination and industry used by Kentuckians, especially at Louisville, to recapture the southern markets.

Salesmen set out from the city in wagons, determined to come back with orders no matter what. There was great rivalry between Louisville and Cincinnati, Ohio, to capture the southern trade and eventually the two great cities found there was enough market for both.

Another great mark of progress was shared by Kentucky and Ohio. In 1866 the first of America's mammoth suspension bridges was completed across the Ohio between Covington and Cincinnati. It stretched for 2,252 feet, and it was conceived by John A. Roebling, who later went on to create the famed Brooklyn Bridge.

The 1870 census showed that the population of Kentucky had reached 1,321,011. In 1875 the first Kentucky Derby was held at Louisville. The next year the Derby had as its most distinguished guest the Emperor of Brazil, Dom Pedro. In 1884 the river communities of the state suffered under one of the worst floods of the Ohio River. Another terror of Nature was the tornado of 1890 which killed 120 people at Louisville. In 1891 the present constitution of the state was adopted. This was the fourth constitution of the commonwealth.

The election for governor in Kentucky in 1899 was one of the strangest and most tragic in the country's history. John Young Brown, William S. Taylor and William Goebel were the candidates. Taylor seemed to have won with a 2,000 vote majority; however, Goebel contested the election, and the matter was brought to the legislature.

On January 30, 1900, Goebel was shot and the legislature immediately selected him as the winner of the election. He had the title for only three days and died on February 3. A period of great confusion followed. Several suspects were placed on trial, and Caleb Powers, secretary of state, was condemned to death; however, all who were convicted were later pardoned, and the real facts of the governor's assassination have never been made known. Lieutenant-Governor J. C. W. Beckham succeeded to the governor's chair.

Another strange series of events during the early 1900's was the so-called "Black-Patch Tobacco War." The Black Patch area of western Kentucky takes its name from the dark tobacco grown there. A Tobacco Trust was trying to force prices down and the tobacco growers formed their own organization to fight this, literally. A group known as the Night Riders or Possum Hunters came into being to "persuade" growers to join. During this period of lawlessness, whippings, burnings, and destruction of tobacco beds were some of the "persuasions" tried. Tobacco prices began to rise, and by 1910 both the Trust and the Night Riders were only memories of the past.

During World War I, 75,043 men from Kentucky saw service. One of the most remarkable records of the war was achieved by Breathitt County. It was the only county in the United States in which no man was drafted during the war. All who left from the county were volunteers.

Another remarkable record was that of Captain Samuel Woodfill, who was named by the commander of American forces, General John Pershing, as the "outstanding figure" of the war.

Up-To-Date

After the war Harlan County, which had been booming, suffered a "bust," and the labor troubles there were among the most severe in the nation. In 1924 Kentucky took a great step forward with the establishment of the first park in its great state park system.

The state's government was almost completely reorganized in 1936, although this was done by amendments instead of by a completely new constitution. Another noteworthy event of 1936 was the completion of the incredible vault at Fort Knox where most of the nation's gold bullion is stored.

The worst flood in the history of the Ohio River in 1937 brought vast hardships to Kentucky. In the lower areas of Louisville only a small part of the downtown was spared the surging floodwaters. In the city alone, losses were more than $50,000,000. Refugees had to be rescued by barge from the second floor windows of the Cobb Hotel in Paducah. Ninety-three per cent of all the buildings in Paducah were unusable. The whole population of Greenup was marooned, and so it went the length of the river. However, after the flood, the energy and determination of the people restored the damaged areas in an unbelievably short time.

During World War II 323,798 men and women saw service from Kentucky. Of these, 4,064 lost their lives in action, and 683 died of wounds. One of those killed was Simon Bolivar Buckner, Jr., native of Munfordville. In 1945 he was the commanding general during the American invasion of Okinawa, where he was killed in action. His father, Simon Bolivar Buckner, Sr., had been a Confederate general.

One of the nation's major efforts to build a modern war force was centered in Kentucky. During this war the role of the tank became particularly important and Fort Knox was the country's primary tank training area.

Postwar Kentucky has shown some remarkable growth—especially in the mushrooming of its cities into great metropolitan areas and in the network of superhighways that lace the state.

Since 1960 one of the state's main themes has been "Make Kentucky a Cleaner, Greener Land"—a drive to keep the state attractive to tourists, and to make it an appealing location for industry. This state was the first to pass anti-billboard legislation, and in 1962 junkyards were forbidden within 2,000 feet of a road unless authorized.

This vigorous effort paid off in 1962 when Kentucky became the first state to win the coveted national Keep America Beautiful award, and the Kentucky program came to serve as the model for other states.

The People of Kentucky

Most of the early settlers of Kentucky were of English, Irish and Scottish origin. Later settlers from France in some numbers were welcomed because of the help France had given to America during the Revolution. Small groups of Swiss arrived over the years. Most of the immigration from Germany occurred between 1848 and 1867. The largest group of foreign-born in the state today are from Germany.

Negroes, both slave and free, arrived with the first settlers, and their talents have brightened the lives of Kentuckians ever since. The striking number of 23,700 Negroes from Kentucky served in the Civil War. Al-

though progress has been slow for Kentucky's 216,000 Negroes, it has been notable in many ways, and the pace is accelerating.

In 1960 Kentucky established a Commission on Human Rights. Orders by Governors Bert T. Combs and Edward T. Breathitt forbade discrimination in employment by the state government and by those who sold goods to or contracted for work by the state. According to some authorities, "the compliance with federal Civil Rights acts marks Kentucky as unusual among states with Southern characteristics." Louisville efforts at desegregation after World War II led to its recognition in 1964 as an "All-American City."

The 1966 legislature enacted into law a landmark Civil Rights bill. Under the historic statue of Abraham Lincoln in the capitol rotunda, Governor Edward T. Breathitt signed this bill into law, thus placing Kentucky in the forefront in the move to give broad civil rights to all minority groups.

"Our Contemporary Ancestors"

After the Scottish, English and Irish peoples first pushed into the mountain regions of Kentucky, they became almost isolated from the rest of the country and kept their habits and customs and even speech, while other areas were changing to more modern ways.

The last few years have seen many changes. Even the most remote mountain cabin is apt now to have a television antenna on its roof and an automobile in the yard. However, much of the age-old tradition of the mountains remains.

On the rocky little farms of the mountains life has been hard; it has been just as hard in the areas around the coal mines and in the mining towns; the abundance that has blessed so much of the rest of the country has in large part passed by the people of the mountains. Yet they continue to retain their quiet pride and independence. They have a fierce pride and loyalty in family, and no one ever suffers want if his family can prevent it. Many are noted for their talent and ingenuity.

From this atmosphere of "splendid isolation" have come customs and attitudes that have long made the region noted.

Much that is picturesque in Kentucky speech is a legacy from the mountain people. Until very recently a large part of their language seemed to come almost directly from the time of Shakespeare and Queen Elizabeth the First.

Not so attractive is the reputation for feuding which has made almost legendary the names of such families as the Hatfields and McCoys. No doubt these struggles came naturally to people who traced their ancestry to the clannish feuds of their Scottish and Irish forebears. However, the mountain family always has been noted for its hospitality to strangers. In many a mountain cabin, the table was never set without an extra place for the visitor who might wander in.

As greater prosperity comes to the mountains and old customs fade, Americans will continue to look to the proud heritage of the mountain people and remember with affection the sunbonnet country with its warm old-fashioned welcome—land of shuckey beans (Leatherbritches) and stack cake, where a bride had to have new shoes if it took all the resources of the community, where when a man died his family and friends would "wagon the deceased to the graveyard," where everyone from the "least-uns to the grandsires" loves music, and where dozens of other customs and sayings will endure in memory long after they have ceased in practice.

Looking back, it will not be hard to realize why today the average Kentuckian still has a reputation for being "unawed and self-reliant."

Collecting Your Thoughts

Select the events in this period of Kentucky history which you think had the greatest meaning for Kentucky's future.

Natural Treasures

Growing Things

As spring slips into Kentucky the state becomes a land of enchanted bloom and color which is probably not equaled anywhere else. The dainty redbud brightens the darkest forest glen and spotlights almost every roadside. The clumps of dogwood hold the eye with their pure gleaming white. Mountain laurel opens its blossoms on the rocky slopes, and flame azalea sweeps like a fire up the mountainside. Among the gleaming dark green foliage, the magnolia blooms spread their waxy petals sometimes as wide as ten inches. Just when it would seem that the spring show could not be topped, the glorious rhododendron burst into flower like exploding fireworks to usher the season from spring to summer.

Smaller plants and wildflowers offer blooms from the last snow to the first frost. The variety of plant life can be demonstrated by the fact that in the Mammoth Cave National Park area alone there are 180 types. Plant life ranges from the semi-Alpine type on the highland crests to the semi-tropical vegetation in the bottoms along the Mississippi River.

One of the romantic and legendary plants of Kentucky is the mistletoe, which grows as a parasite on trees. Children are often told they may pick it from any tree except an oak. The Druids are said to hold the mistletoe to its place on an oak. If the Druid's grasp is broken it might bring disaster to the "hull relation."

When Europeans first came to the Kentucky region, they found it an area of unsurpassed forests covering three-fourths of the present area of the state. Even today forests blanket 11,497,000 acres or 45 per cent of Kentucky's total land area. More than 70 species of trees are native to Kentucky, including such unusual ones as mockernut and pignut hickory, hornbeam and hop hornbeam, chinquapin oak, overcup oak, swamp chestnut oak and persimmon.

An interesting tree is Franklinia, named for Benjamin Franklin, who identified it. Specimens of this tree are found in Cave Hill Cemetery at Louisville. This cemetery is one of the country's best-known botanical gardens, with a wide variety of trees and plants. The campus of the University of Louisville is also noted for its rare trees, including a tree appropriately known as the Chinese scholar, as well as zelkova, Siberian elms with exfoliating bark, cerdidephyllum, golden raintree, and ornamental ginkgo.

Another outstanding nature area is Bernheim Forest, near Louisville, which has, perhaps, the widest assortment of flora and fauna in the state. It is privately endowed and open free to the public.

Kentucky is one of the few states to have "a tree that owns itself." A group of people at Pippa Passes admired a sycamore tree so much that they bought the 36 square feet of land on which the tree stands, and gave the tree its own land as a gift; the deed is on record in Knott County.

Living Creatures

The vast numbers of buffalo that once roamed the forest paths of Kentucky are no more; the stealthy panther or mountain lion no longer snarls his defiance in the state; the unbelievable clouds of passenger pigeons are only a distant memory. The dainty, darting Louisiana parakeet and the demure-looking prairie chicken have also disappeared. Many of the 300 species of birds recorded in the state are no longer seen, but numerous other creatures of Nature have managed to survive and even flourish in the woodland depths or hedgerows of the state.

Deer, rabbits, squirrels, and ruffed grouse are particular favorites of hunters in season. Pennyrile Forest is an especial favorite of deer hunters. A unique opportunity for hunters is the primitive Weapons Hunting Area inside the Cumberland National Forest in Bath and Menifee counties. Here hunters test their skill with longbows, crossbows, muzzle-loading rifles and muzzle-loading shotguns. This section is one of the few in the nation where crossbows are legal.

A misty dawn in November will find eager pink-coated fox hunters and even more eager dogs assembled for one of the state's famous fox hunts. There are three major hunts in Kentucky—Carlisle, Iroquois at Grimes Mill near Lexington, and Louisville. The chase carries the snorting horses over many a rail fence and through enchanted woodland. Fox hunts are popular almost everywhere in the state, and less formal ones may find a mountain man in overalls eagerly following as fine a fox hound as any belonging to the aristocratic club members.

From Kentucky's earliest days the Southern tradition of night hunting has also been a part of many rural communities. For the night hunt, dog owners sit around a campfire to listen for the sounds of their Walker and Trigg hounds; a change in the sound will tell them that the raccoon has been treed. The famous Walker strain of dogs was developed in Madison County and the Trigg strain in the community of Glasgow.

Among Kentucky's strangest natural creatures are those found in Mammoth Cave. Ages of darkness in the cave have produced blind crickets, crawfish and sightless fish, with their sense of touch greatly increased. Bodies of the fish (amblyopsis spaeleus) are so transparent that their skeletons may be seen. These were the first cave creatures ever studied thoroughly.

In regard to other fish, more than 200 varieties now swim the many waters of Kentucky. "They bite every day of the year," is the boast of the state's fishermen. The bass population in Lake Cumberland is said to be denser than in any other large lake in the United States. Other popular fish include walleye, sucker and buffalo, crappie, bluegill, muskie, sauger and rainbow trout.

Mineral Treasures

Kentucky's unbelievable reserves of coal have scarcely been touched. A recent survey revealed that sixty-seven billion tons of coal still remain in the ground. Clays, barite, fluorspar, gem stones (including agate, flint, fluorite and sphalerite), lead, zinc, sand, gravel and stone (including limestone and sandstone), oil and natural gas are among the other minerals found.

Collecting Your Thoughts

Many state departments and private organizations are devoted to preserving the natural features of Kentucky so that they may be enjoyed for all time. Find out something about conservation practices in the state.

People Use Their Treasures

Royalty on Four Feet

One of the most heartwarming sights anywhere is common in Kentucky. Hardly a visitor fails to be moved by the appealing foals venturing away from their mothers to frolic on the lush grasses or, becoming timid again, tagging along meekly behind the proud but placid mares. In another mood, mares, colts and fillies may all playfully kick up their heels and dash across the meadows, giving a hint of their great speed.

As early as 1775, Daniel Boone proposed to the Virginia Legislature a resolution to improve the breed of horses in Kentucky. Ever since that time, one of the most intense interests of the state has been to develop the world's finest horses. The bluegrass, which grows on a rich limestone base, contains limestone and other chemicals which seem to be just right for this purpose.

Because of this, the 1,200 square miles of land around Lexington, "the horse-center of America," and some other parts of the state must be ranked among the most cherished real estate of the globe. Around Lexington alone are more than 200 fine horse farms, and there are more than 250 in the state. They have also been described as the "most beautiful farms in the world."

On many of these, stately white-columned mansions loom at the end of long winding lanes across blue-green fields, enclosed by white board fences. Board fencing is used because the valuable animals are very prone to injure themselves against wire fences. However, the beauty of mile after mile of the white planking seems to make the expense worthwhile in itself. Some of the most famous of these individual farms are discussed in a later section.

All types of horses are raised in Kentucky. Probably the most familiar is the thoroughbred; only horses whose ancestry can be traced to certain original horses are considered thoroughbreds. Harness racing horses are called standard-breds. Kentucky has about 75 standard-bred farms. The third most important type of Kentucky horse is the saddlebred—trained to display its ability at horse shows and to rank among the world's finest riding horses. The most prominent saddlebred breeding place in

Kentucky, and probably in the world, is Dodge Stables, at Castleton Farm.

Quarter horses, appaloosas, palominos, pure-blooded Arabians, and ponies of many types round out the full-scale nature of the horse industry in Kentucky.

The raising, selling, showing and racing of horses is a business of importance in Kentucky. In 1964 public auction sales of horses in the state totaled almost $ 20,000,000. This does not include private sales throughout the state. Such wealthy owners as Mr. and Mrs. John W. Galbreath of the Darby Dan Farm are willing to pay vast sums for fine horses, such as their $2,000,000 purchase of Swaps. Just one horse— Kelso—earned $1,893,362 in 56 races. The sons and daughters of just one stallion, Bull Lea of Calumet Farms, earned $13,000,000 in race tracks across the world. One of these offspring was the famed Citation, winner of the 1948 Kentucky Derby.

Probably the most famous horse of all time was the "super-horse" Man o'War, bought for only $5,000 by Samuel Riddle of Faraway Farm. This horse's best-known son was War Admiral, winner of the three races that make up the so-called "Triple Crown" of racing—the Kentucky Derby, the Preakness and the Belmont. An earlier Kentucky horse of great fame was appropriately named Lexington. So famous did he become that his skeleton is exhibited in the Smithsonian Institution in Washington as one of the finest of his breed.

One of the interesting problems of horsemen is the naming of their thoroughbreds. Every year all foals (as newborn horses are called) are registered in the American Stud Book. So many thousands of names are registered there that great ingenuity and imagination are needed to come up with new names. One man was asked why he had named his horse Bad News; he replied that he hoped the horse would live up to the general reputation that bad news travels fast. Sometimes a human baby is "saddled" with an equine name. One racing enthusiast promised to name his expected baby for the Kentucky Derby winner. When his twins arrived, they were known as Baggenbaggage and Bubbling Over Jones.

A Burley Crop

Kentucky's most valuable crop came about as a happy accident during the Civil War when a Bracken County farmer saved a few seeds from a particularly light-colored plant in his tobacco plot. He and a few other planters began cultivating the new strain, and in 1867 this strain won first and second prizes at the St. Louis Fair. This was called burley tobacco, and today Kentucky is the world's number one producer of burley tobacco. Little burley tobacco is grown anywhere else in the world. The high phosphate content of Kentucky soil seems to be ideal for this. Every year sales of burley bring more than $325,000,000 to Kentucky tobacco farmers. Nearly half of all Kentucky agricultural receipts comes from tobacco. Altogether, Kentucky ranks second among the states in total tobacco sales. All of the world's Green River dark air cured tobacco is produced around the Owensboro area. This is used in chewing tobacco.

Growing of tobacco requires great care, and one acre of tobacco demands as much as 488 man-hours to bring the crop to successful harvest. One-family tobacco operations can cover no more than 10 to 12 acres, and even this requires almost constant effort. The seedbed has to be prepared and then burned over to destroy weeds and parasites; seeds are planted in frames to protect them from cold; the beds are covered with muslin; the tender plants are reset in the fields after a couple of months, following fertilizing and harrowing of the ground. Suckers on the plants are removed by hand, as are any worms that show up.

The tender leaf stalks are cut by hand and threaded on a stick, no more than six to a stick. After being brought carefully to the barns to avoid bruises, the sticks of tobacco are hung vertically several inches apart to cure. After curing, the tobacco is sorted by grades into "hands" and taken to market. Tobacco auctions are fascinating places; the graded hands of cured tobacco leaf are piled in flat baskets standing up to five feet high and weighing as much as 600 pounds. With tobacco buyers from all over the world following, the auctioneer moves from basket to basket chanting an almost incomprehensible sing-song bidding ritual for each sale.

TOBACCO

Thirty tobacco market centers in Kentucky operate from November to February to sell the year's tobacco crop to the highest bidders. The world's largest loose leaf auction market is in Lexington.

Tobacco has been a leading business in the state since 1825 when the first market to sell tobacco in hogsheads began operation at Louisville. At one time tobacco was legal tender, and fine tobacco was even used as a "ransom" for brides. By 1865 Kentucky had taken the lead in United States tobacco production, and it has held first or second position almost ever since.

Other Accomplishments in Agriculture

Total income from agriculture in Kentucky in 1964 was $732,663,000. Crops accounted for $418,918,000 and livestock for $313,745,000. Kentucky is one of the few states in which livestock receipts are lower than those from crops. Of these totals, grain crops and dairy products each bring in about $100,000,000. Kentucky is now the nation's third largest producer of American cheese, and it ranks second in producing evaporated milk. A whole new industry has been created in poultry—the raising of broilers.

Kentucky ranks first in production of tall fescue seed and lespedeza and second in Kentucky bluegrass seed and orchard grass seed. At one time bluegrass seed had to be harvested by hand; now seed harvesters are manufactured in Winchester. Cleaning the seeds is an interesting process and several seed cleaning plants at Paris produce hundreds of thousands of bushels of bluegrass seed each year. Many people are disappointed when they see the bluegrass area because it is not "blue." The bluegrass takes on its bluish tone only when it is coming into its tiny bloom in May.

In early days hemp was a leading Kentucky crop. Rope braided from Kentucky hemp supplied the ropes for the navy sailing ships until steam power displaced sails. "Senging" or the gathering of ginseng root was another activity that has almost passed. A digger who had brought in the most root during the season looked forward to being awarded a small prize. Ginseng was valued highly by the Chinese for medicine and other uses.

Many Kentucky families still keep their own smokehouses, where the delicious Kentucky aged hams are produced. This is said by some to be "the most delicious meat in the world."

Kentucky has long supplied a large part of the finest hardwood timber on the North American continent. Almost all of the forest land of the state is suitable for commercial timber, amounting to a total of 46 per cent of the land surface. Value of timber products is about $260,000,000 per year. Oaks, birch, maple, sweetgum, hickory, yellow poplar, ash, cottonwood, white pine, shortleaf and lobloly pine, hemlock and cypress are the main commercial woods.

Manufacturing

Someone has said that manufactured products of Kentucky range the alphabet from acetylene to yoghurt. The value of manufacturing in the state amounted to $2,446,000,000 in 1963. The value of manufacturing in the Louisville area alone reached almost a billion and a half dollars in 1964, making the city the largest manufacturing center of the southeast.

Food processors are the largest income producing industries. Others are electrical machinery, tobacco processing, petroleum, chemicals, other machinery, and apparel.

People in Kentucky began distilling whiskey as early as 1789, in Georgetown. When Jacob Spears and his associates started to make whiskey at Paris in 1790, they called their product Bourbon, in honor of their county. The combination of Kentucky grains and pure spring water produced a product that was much admired, and Kentucky continues to produce the world's largest quantities of Bourbon whiskey. Much of the work is done by hand to maintain the quality. The various Kentucky formulas for Bourbon whiskey are among the world's most carefully kept industrial secrets.

An even earlier Kentucky industry was iron making, which began at Pilot Knob in 1798. The iron makers came to be ranked among the aristocrats of the state. When a new furnace was opened, there was a holiday. The first fire was lit with ceremony, and there were banquets; when the pig iron was poured into molds, young couples pressed their

initials into the soft metal; dancing followed through much of the night.

Even though there is not enough iron ore in Kentucky for commercial use, steel making is still a major Kentucky industry. The world's largest steel blast furnace is a part of the Armco Steel Corporation's mill at Ashland. Ashland is known as the "steel-making, oil refining, industrial hub of eastern Kentucky."

In a more sophisticated metal industry the gaseous diffusion uranium processing plant of Paducah is one of only three such plants in the entire United States.

Another Kentucky product carries a lot of power. Louisville is the home of the famous Louisville Slugger baseball bats; its manufacturers, Hillerich and Bradsby Company, are the largest bat manufacturers in the world, and their bats are standard in the major leagues. Hawesville is known as the sorghum-making capital of the world, and sorghum (molasses) has been produced in Kentucky since before the days of mule-powered sorghum mills. The world's largest knit goods plant is located at Campbellsville.

Since the early river days, Kentucky has been a leader in boat building, with Paducah a present-day center of boat building and repairing. Because of its fine woods, Kentucky is well-known for its furniture making—especially for its cabin furniture.

Cabin and home industries have had an important place in making Kentucky people independent. The State Department of Commerce has a division of craft development which helps the state's fine craftsmen create better products and helps to provide a market for their goods. Crafts range from the gee-haw-whinny-diddle toy, whittled from rhododendron, and the corn-shuck dolls first made by the Indians, to the fine hooked rugs and beautiful weaving of such individuals and groups as the Churchill Weavers of Berea. This group was founded by D. C. Churchill, and to make their noted textiles they use the unusual hand looms which he devised. Other leaders in the effort to encourage and improve the home industries were Mr. and Mrs. A. E. Barnes. They produced homespun and home-woven scarves, coverlets, runners and other materials in authentic old designs.

Handcrafts bring in only about $1,300,000 a year, but this is income that provides a great boost to some of the families that need it the most.

One of Kentucky's most exotic products resulted from the hunters' skill. Most of the tall headdresses (called shakos) used by Napoleon's armies came from bears of the Kentucky hills.

Mining and Mineral Products

In 1964 Kentucky ranked 14th among mineral producing states. Mineral products bring about $440,000,000 of income into the state each year. The remark is often made in Kentucky that its mining is "old as the hills."

One of the state's most persistent and compelling legends concerns the mining activities of John Swift. The story is told that Swift and his men worked a silver mine from 1760 until 1769. Whenever they could not take their silver out because of Indian threats or the weather, they are supposed to have hidden it away. As far as is known, none of this hidden treasure has ever been found. Almost every eastern Kentucky county claims to be the location of Swift's hidden wealth, but most indications are that it was in the Paint Creek area of Johnson County. Treasure seekers have never ceased to search for this tantalizing hoard.

Today, of course, coal is king of Kentucky mining. The state ranks second in the nation in bituminous coal mining. In 1965 a celebration was held to recognize the 3 billionth ton of coal mined in Kentucky. Some of Kentucky's mines are among the most modern in the country. There is a strange contrast between a completely automated coal mine and the primitive hill farms which may be nearby.

Muhlenberg County, in the Western Coal Field, is the state's largest coal producer. In this region most of the work is done by strip mining, where the surface soil is scraped away and the layers of coal are stripped from the top without any need for tunnels or pits. Because strip mining has destroyed the beauty of many Kentucky hillsides and mountains, the 1966 Legislature enacted a bill requiring strip mine proprietors to restore or reclaim the land after stripping it of coal.

One of the earliest oil wells ever drilled was brought in by accident near Burkesville in 1829. Dr. John Croghan had a crew drilling for salt water to be used in making salt by evaporation. When the workers withdrew the drill one day, oil gushed out. It continued to flow until the surface of the Cumberland River was covered; when a spark struck the surface, flames raged up, terrorizing those in the neighborhood. Poor Dr. Croghan was ruined by this muddy looking black stuff which kept him from getting his valuable salt, and the oil was unused since it seemed to be good for nothing. Finally someone discovered that it might be used in making certain kinds of medicines.

Today Kentucky ranks 16th among the petroleum producing states, but enough oil is produced to make oil second to coal among Kentucky minerals. In 1964 nearly 19,000 producing oil wells in 67 counties pumped over 19,700,000 barrels of crude oil with an estimated value of nearly $60,000,000. Near Catlettsburg, Ashland Oil Company built the world's first plant for producing naphthalene from petroleum in commercial quantities.

The first natural gas was produced in Kentucky in 1858. Natural gas production, mostly in western Kentucky, runs to about 74 billion cubic feet annually from more than 4,000 wells; reserves are estimated at over 1,000 billion cubic feet. More than 90 of the state's 120 counties have large supplies of natural gas.

Nearly half of the nation's supply of fluorspar is produced along the lower Ohio River above Paducah. Veins mined recently in the Kentucky River area of central Kentucky produce barite and associated minerals. Limestone is mined and crushed at 111 quarries. Dolomite is produced in a three-county area around Louisville. Kentucky is becoming more and more important as a source of silica sand for glass making.

Kentucky ranks second among the states in ball clay production. Mines in Carter and Rowan counties produce clays for firebricks and block and other clay products; other counties produce clay for floor and wall tile. A total of 280,000 tons of clay is mined each year in the state.

Transportation and Communication

". . . On the unexpected arrival of the boat before Louisville, in the course of a fine, still, moonlight night, the extraordinary sound which filled the air, as the pent-up steam was suffered to escape from the valves on rounding to, produced a general alarm, and multitudes rose from their beds to ascertain the cause. I have heard that the general impression among the Kentuckians was that a comet had fallen into the Ohio."

This was one man's comment about the first steamboat as it arrived in Kentucky. The effect of steamboating on the Ohio was more like a meteor than a comet. The number of boats increased at an incredible rate, carrying the goods and passengers of the entire Ohio-Mississippi valley, in one of the most "glamorous" periods of Kentucky history.

Boats grew larger until they were "floating palaces," with luxurious carpeting, crystal chandeliers, string orchestras, beautifully set tables and unending courses of food. There were showboats bringing the latest theater to the river towns, and even floating stores that carried merchandise for sale to those who hurried down to the cobblestone landings.

There was a great rage for steamboat racing. "I think the most enjoyable of all races is a steamboat race. . . ." said Mark Twain. "Two red-hot steamboats raging along, neck and neck, straining every nerve . . . quaking . . . and groaning from stem to stern, spouting white steam

from the pipes, pouring black smoke from the chimneys . . . parting the river into long streaks of hissing foam—this is sport that makes a body's very liver curl with enjoyment." Twain did not mention, however, that there were many disasters in steamboat racing, with boats blowing up or crashing as they strained to win.

Even before the steamboat, the Ohio was a busy river. Countless settlers drifted down the river on rafts and flatboats to their homes. Goods were floated down river to the markets of Louisiana. The boatmen became known as the most rough and ready characters of the country.

Today the steamboats are almost gone, but more tonnage goes up the Ohio than ever before in barges propelled by sturdy diesel towboats. Because Kentucky has more miles of navigable waterways than any other state but Alaska, river transportation is especially important to the state. There are 1,300 miles of inland waterways. One of the most unusual of these is the Green River with its narrow but deep channel.

The first "highways" of Kentucky were the paths of the buffalo. Indians followed these trails for hundreds of miles. Footsteps of Iroquois, Miami, Cherokee, Shawnee, Creek, Catawba, and others made a famous route called the Warrior's Trace. It carried them through the Cumberland Gap.

MODERN TOWBOAT

MOUNTAIN PARKWAY

Dr. Thomas Walker and other Europeans followed the old buffalo and Indian traces. Daniel Boone blazed the famous Boone's Trace. Benjamin Logan blazed the even more famous Wilderness Road, starting from Boone's Trace and eventually reaching the Falls of the Ohio at present Louisville.

Today these rough and rocky stretches have been transformed into a highway system stretching for 21,000 miles, including the magnificent Mountain Parkway, the Bluegrass Parkway and Western Kentucky Parkway as well as several sections of the Interstate Highway system. Lexington has become an important intersection of major expressways.

In 1832 one of the first railroads west of the mountains was operating between Frankfort and Lexington. This railroad used mules and horses for its power. Modern Kentucky has about 3,500 miles of railroad; one major railroad, the Louisville and Nashville, has headquarters in Kentucky. Railroad fans travel long distances to visit Clearfield, where one of the nation's few remaining steam-powered railroads, the Morehead and North Fork, runs over its four-mile-long route.

John Bradford bought an ancient printing press at Philadelphia. With great labor this was brought over the mountains to Pittsburgh and floated down the Ohio on a flatboat to Maysville, then carried by pack horse to Lexington. There Bradford, who had no previous experience in printing or newspaper work, produced Kentucky's first newspaper—the Kentucky *Gazette*—on August 11, 1787. Bradford became a success and later published pamphlets and even books.

The first daily newspaper to be published in the United States west of the mountains was the Louisville *Advertiser,* started in 1826.

The world's most famous braille printing company is the American Printing House for the Blind in Louisville. It was begun with private funds but now receives a subsidy from the federal government for the important work it does in helping blind people obtain reading material.

Collecting Your Thoughts

Many activities in Kentucky succeeded because conditions were just right for them. Make as long a list as you can of these.

Human Treasures

Mr. President

"I was born February 12, 1809, in then Hardin County, Kentucky, at a point within the now recently formed county of Larue, a mile, or a mile and a half from where Hodginsville (sic) now is," wrote the great Civil War President, Abraham Lincoln, as he recalled his birthplace. Kentucky has been the home of two Presidents of the United States and birthplace of the only President of the Confederate States.

Abraham Lincoln, grandfather of the President, moved from Virginia to land near the Green River sometime between 1782 and 1784. Later he moved his family to a cabin near Simpsonville, where he was killed by an Indian. His son Mordecai was able to kill the invader before he killed other members of the family, including his youngest brother, Thomas Lincoln.

In 1803 Abraham Lincoln's widow, Bersheba, and her son Thomas moved to a farm six miles northwest of Elizabethtown, where they lived with Thomas' sister and her husband. Before he was married, Thomas Lincoln is said to have built a mill and millrace on Valley Creek in Elizabethtown. He was interested in Sarah Bush, but she married Daniel Johnston. Later Thomas Lincoln married Nancy Hanks. Lincoln and Nancy Hanks moved to a 348-acre farm; Sinking Spring, near Hodgenville. Here he built a one-room log cabin, 12 feet wide, 17 feet long and 11 logs high. Their first child, Sarah, was born here and then a son, Abraham.

When Abraham was four years old, the Thomas Lincoln family moved to another farm, near Elizabethtown. Of this, Lincoln said "My earliest recollections are of the Knob Creek Place." Here Abraham probably had some short periods of very poor schooling. The Lincolns shopped at the Green-Helm store in Elizabethtown. When Lincoln met Judge John B. Helm 40 years later, he introduced the Judge as "the first man I ever knew who wore store clothes all the week . . . who fed me on maple sugar, when as a small boy I sat upon a nail keg in his uncle's store."

Thomas Lincoln had difficulty in getting a clear title to his Knob Creek land, so in 1816 he decided to move to Indiana where the federal land survey made titles more certain.

David R. Murray, who had been a boy at Cloverport when they ferried the Ohio there, wrote in later life: "On account of the unusual size of the oxen, a crowd soon gathered to find out who these people were and where they were going. . . . Old Minerva, a colored slave, who had been attracted to the scene, seeing the condition of the children, went back into the house and came back immediately with a plate heaped with slices of homemade bread covered with butter, a pitcher of milk, and some cups. . . . In those days there were no ferry boats, and passengers, whenever any came along, were set across in a canoe. When the Lincolns reached the ferry, a raft was made, with the assistance of several people, and the wagon placed upon it. With one man in the canoe to pull and one man on the rear of the raft to push with a long pole (the river was low at the time), the Lincolns were ferried across to the Indiana shore and landed. The two oxen and the cow were made to swim over."

When Nancy Hanks Lincoln died, Thomas Lincoln returned to marry his first love, Sarah Bush Johnston, then a widow, who became the much loved step-mother of the future president. Abraham Lincoln, himself, also found a wife from Kentucky. Mary Todd had been born in 1818 in Lexington. When her mother died, she went to Springfield, Illinois, to live with her sister. There she met and eventually married Abraham Lincoln.

An interesting minor episode in Lincoln's life occurred in Lewisport. From the Indiana shore he had rowed out to the middle of the Ohio to take a passenger to a boat which could not come to shore. He was brought before the Judge at Lewisport and charged with violating the rights of the ferrymen in the area. Although only eighteen years old, he had read much about the law so he served as his own attorney and was acquitted.

Jefferson Davis, the man who was to become Lincoln's principal opposite as President of the Confederate States of America, was born at Fairview only about 100 miles from Lincoln's birthplace. Both men were born less than a year apart. Oddly, too, they both served in the Black Hawk War.

BOONE   DAVIS   TAYLOR   LINCOLN

Jefferson Davis attended Transylvania University, Lexington, then went to West Point, where he graduated. As the argument over slavery grew more fierce, Jefferson Davis became known as one of the strongest supporters of the states against the national government. He was almost a unanimous choice for President of the Confederacy.

When the Confederate cause was lost, Jefferson Davis hoped to escape to Europe, but he was captured and served two years in federal prisons. The remainder of his life was spent quietly at his Mississippi home. He died at New Orleans in 1889, and his birthday has become a public holiday in most Southern states.

Zachary Taylor was born in Virginia on November 24, 1784, but he was only nine months old when his parents brought him to Kentucky where he was raised. Colonel Richard Taylor, Zachary's father, built his first log house in Kentucky. Zachary Taylor's greatest fame before becoming the 12th President of the United States was as the hero of the Mexican War. "Old Rough and Ready" defeated Santa Anna at Buena Vista and broke the power of the Mexican army. His daughter, Knoxie, married Jefferson Davis, although her father was very much opposed to the marriage. Zachary Taylor became ill and died July 9, 1850, having served as President only one year, four months and four days. He is buried in the family cemetery near Louisville.

Our "First" Frontiersman

The beginnings of Kentucky are so closely tied to Daniel Boone that few people can think of one without the other. Boone was a simple man who probably would be surprised and shocked at the legends that have grown up around his name. That his life story would be told in fiction every week on television, that books and motion pictures without end would be concerned with his life would have been unbelievable to him, and yet even during his lifetime he had become a legend.

This is not surprising. The simple facts of his life are almost incredible. In his long lifetime he grew to know America intimately from Florida to

Ohio, from Virginia to western Missouri. He was captured by the Indians, not once but several times. In 1778 the Indians carried him as a prisoner to Detroit. Because his knowledge of the wilderness was so great, admiring Chief Black Fish adopted him as his own son, but Boone escaped and made his way back to Boonesborough to save it from attack.

In spite of his modesty, Boone could not seem to keep from carving his name on Kentucky trees. Most of these have disappeared, but one of the prized possessions of the Filson Club in Louisville is the trunk of a tree with this carving: "D Boone Kill a Bar 1803 ZOIS." This had been cut down at Iroquois Park in Louisville in 1932.

In spite of his fame, Boone was never very successful or happy in life's work. He had to defend himself, successfully, against a charge of conspiracy brought by Colonel Calloway. As early as 1771 Boone and his brother "Bible" Boone were returning home to Virginia with the furs they had taken in two years of hunting. At Cumberland Gap the Cherokee confiscated all of the furs and the brothers had to return empty-handed.

Much later, heavily in debt, unable to obtain clear title to the lands he claimed, and not very successful as a tavern keeper at Maysville, Daniel Boone left Kentucky, paddling his way up the Ohio in a canoe he had hollowed out of a tree trunk. For a time he made his home in West Virginia, and then at the age of sixty-five went to live in Missouri where some of his family lived and the Spanish government had given him a generous grant of land. Later this was attached by his Kentucky creditors, and the old Pathfinder had to go back to trapping furs to pay his debts.

When Daniel Boone and his wife died, their bodies were brought back to Kentucky, even though Boone had said he never wished to return to the land of his early fame. Kentucky now honors her famous trail blazer.

Other Public Figures

In addition to Presidents, Kentucky has produced four vice presidents, a chief justice of the United States, and seven associate justices of the

United States Supreme Court.

Richard M. Johnson, 1780–1850, was vice president under Martin Van Buren from 1837 to 1841. A hero of the Indian wars, he established the Choctaw Indian Academy near Georgetown. John C. Breckinridge was vice president under James Buchanan. This Lexington native was a candidate for President in 1860 under the banner of the Southern wing of the Democratic Party. Another vice president bears the name made more famous in a later day by his grandson. Adlai E. Stevenson, 1835–1914, was a native of Christian County and vice president under Grover Cleveland. Most famous political figure in recent Kentucky history was Vice President Alben Barkley, born in Graves County, later making his home in Paducah. While serving under President Harry Truman, he became noted as the "Veep," as a nickname for the initials V. P. (Vice President).

One of the best-known political figures in the United States, aside from its Presidents, was Henry Clay, Kentucky's representative in the Hall of Fame at the national capitol. Although not born in Kentucky, he made his home at Ashland. He made his first speech from a huge stump at Winchester. In 1832, a steamboat carrying Henry Clay made a wrong turn and went up the Salt River, making him miss an important speech. Some say that this may have cost him the presidential nomination and the presidency. To this day, Kentuckians say that a losing candidate "has gone up Salt River."

A native of Louisa, Fred M. Vinson served as Chief Justice of the United States until 1953. One of the most famous of all Supreme Court justices was Louis Dembitz Brandeis, born in Louisville. Another Kentucky justice was John Marshall Harlan.

A notable fact is that 41 natives of Kentucky became generals in the Union Army during the Civil War and 38 natives were Confederate generals. Probably no other state can nearly match this total. Famous Kentucky military men include General John Hunt Morgan of Hopemont, General John B. Hood, perhaps most famous for his defense of Atlanta against Sherman, General Ambrose E. Burnside, General William Orlando Butler, General Albert Sidney Johnston, and General Benjamin Hardin Helm. General Henry W. Lawton, captor of the notorious Indian leader Geronimo, later died a hero in the Philippines during the Spanish-American War. Confederate General Simon Bolivar Buckner, Sr., surrendered to General Grant. The healing effect of time is shown by the fact that when President Grant died, Buckner was chosen as one of his pallbearers.

Almost as well-known are Kentucky colonels. Many prominent people have been given the honorary title of Kentucky Colonel. Now there is a new honorary rank—Admiral of the Commonwealth, a title given to those who have helped to promote the waterways and travel of the state. Such diverse personalities as President Lyndon B. Johnson, hotelman Conrad Hilton, actor Ernest Borgnine and this writer are Kentucky Admirals.

Innovators

Two most unfortunate inventors were associated with Kentucky. John Fitch, now recognized as the inventor of the steamboat, ended his life at Bardstown, when he found he could get neither a living nor recognition for his work. William "Pig-Iron" Kelly of Kuttawa developed an improved method for making steel. English inventor Sir Henry Bessemer was given a United States patent on a similar process, but Kelly convinced the patent office that he had prior rights and he was given the patent instead of Bessemer. However, Bessemer's name continued to be linked with the process, and Kelly has never been given the recognition he deserves.

Nathan Stubblefield, pioneer of radio transmission, is said by some to be the first person ever to transmit a human voice by "wireless," in the small town of Murray in 1892. Later a St. Louis newspaper said, "However undeveloped his system may be, Nathan B. Stubblefield, the farmer inventor of Kentucky, has accurately discovered the principle of telephoning without wires."

John McAdam, father of a new road surfacing method, gave his name to the macadam road. Thomas Harris Barlow began the Barlow Planetarium. John B. Bibb developed a gourmet's delight—Bibb lettuce in his garden at Frankfort. Dr. Walter Brashear performed the first successful hip joint amputation.

In 1809 Dr. Ephraim McDowell of Danville had a patient, Mrs. Jane

Crawford, who needed a serious operation. He told her that he had never done this operation, but that he felt he could. Mrs. Crawford, in great pain, rode horseback the 60 miles to his office and there without anesthetic (which had not yet been invented) Dr. McDowell performed the first ovariotomy done in America. Mrs. Crawford recited the Psalms to keep her mind from the pain while men held her arms and legs to keep her quiet. She recovered rapidly and lived for many years.

Creative Kentuckians

One of America's most beloved humorists, Irvin S. Cobb, was born in Paducah. Two of his best-known books were *The Life of the Party* and his autobiography, *Exit Laughing.* Through his motion pictures, such as *Judge Priest,* he became known to millions who might not have read his books.

Another well-loved Kentucky author was Alice Hegan Rice, probably best-known for her *Mrs. Wiggs of the Cabbage Patch.* Part of the Cabbage Patch settlement which inspired the story is still in Louisville. Still other books by a Kentucky author, considered by many with fond sentiment, are *The Little Shepherd of Kingdom Come* and *The Trail of the Lonesome Pine* by John Fox, Jr., born near Paris.

Other writers that have made Kentucky proud are novelist Elizabeth Madox Roberts; A. B. (Bud) Guthrie, author of *The Big Sky;* Jesse Stuart; Annie Fellows Johnston, who wrote *The Little Colonel* series; James Lane Allen; poet Madison Cawein; contemporary poet Hallis Summers; the great literary scholar, Robert Penn Warren, author of *All the King's Men, World Enough and Time* and numerous authoritative literary texts and winner of two Pulitzer Prizes; and Cleanth Brooks, another eminent scholarly writer.

Henry Watterson, famed Kentucky editor, was awarded the Pulitzer Prize for journalism in 1917. A book which gained much fame was written by Thomas Merton, known as Father M. Louis of Abbey of Our Lady of Gethsemane. This was *The Seven Storey Mountain.*

According to the Kentucky Department of Public Information, "one man, John Jacob Niles, folk singer, armed with guitar and dulcimer, has done more than any other in the United States to popularize the archaic beauty of Appalachian folk songs. Trekking mountain trails, Niles has learned and transcribed the half-forgotten ballads from the lips of singers, and has himself composed many songs in this idiom."

About 1808 a young man began strolling about the Kentucky countryside, observing nature and sketching. He remained in Kentucky for almost eighteen years, operated a general store and mill at Henderson, and kept a frog and turtle pond as part of his study of wild life. The man was John James Audubon—probably the most renowned artist of natural history who ever lived. A gifted modern-day Kentucky naturalist-artist is Ray Harm of the University of Kentucky.

Other Kentucky artists of note include William Edward, internationally known portraitist; Matthew H. Jouett, in early days called "the best painter west of the Appalachians;" Frank Duveneck, painter, sculptor, etcher, and teacher, who is said to have become an "overnight sensation;" and George Brewer. Brewer created his art to promote Mammoth Cave, and he sometimes worked in the cave with 500 oil lamps to throw light on the weird beauty of his subject.

David Wark Griffith, born at La Grange, gained fame as one of the outstanding producers of motion pictures. His *Birth of a Nation* is considered the first truly great movie.

Such Interesting People

Dan Carter Beard, native of Covington, organized a group of boys in a club which he called Sons of Daniel Boone; the boys learned how to make dugout canoes and other items, how to take care of themselves in the woods, and other skills. When Lord Baden-Powell formed the first Boy Scout group in England, he patterned much of his organization on Beard's Sons of Daniel Boone. Later, Beard merged his group to form the American Boy Scouts. The first troop in the country was organized by Beard at Burnside.

Every year the Kentucky air resounds to the sounds of cornstalk fiddlers, gourd banjos, and homemade dulcimers as the American Folk Song Festival continues in the tradition established by Jean Thomas of Ashland. Jean Thomas became known as the "Traipsin' Woman"

because of her many travels through the mountains studying folk customs and culture. Among her many other popular and scholarly contributions to folk culture, she started the popular Folk Song Festival held each year at Ashland. An interesting sidelight of her life is that she was the press agent for the famed singer Texas Guinan during the roaring 20's.

Other varied Kentucky personalities include Kit Carson, born near Richmond; Carrie Nation, a native of Garrard County; almost legendary trainman John Luther (Casey) Jones, born at Jordan; William Holmes McGuffey, who began his noted series of readers while teaching at Paris; Colonel Matt Winn, who took over Churchill Downs in 1902 and made it one of the best-known race courses in the world; and Mrs. Kingsley Walker who for 34 years has made the wreath of roses for each Kentucky Derby winner.

Still others are Mrs. C. V. Whitney, world social leader, of Lexington; Mary Breckinridge, founder and promoter of the invaluable Frontier Nursing Service; Fathers Nerincx and Theodore Badin, founders of Catholicism in Kentucky; Dr. William James Hutchins, internationally known educator and an early president of Berea College; James D. Porter, the Kentucky Giant, who stood 7 feet, 9 inches tall; and Colonel Harland Sanders, of Corbin, who has come to be known as America's "Fried Chicken King."

Collecting Your Thoughts

Something about the land of Kentucky is said to produce people who are brave, self-reliant and ingenious. List some Kentuckians who seem to fit such a description.

Teaching and Learning

Because of the unique needs of its mountain people, Kentucky has developed some unusual educational institutions. One of the most notable of these is Berea College at Berea. Students come from both the mountain byways and from city high schools. For those older students with problems in reading or other subjects in which they may have lacked training, special courses are given. The culture and crafts of the mountain region are preserved and promoted here. An unusual program of art and music is keyed to the resources of the surrounding mountains.

Most Berea students work in businesses and industries owned by the college to pay a large part of their expenses. There was no segregation at Berea until required by Kentucky law in 1904. At that time, Berea helped to establish Lincoln Institute for Negroes.

BEREA

The University of Kentucky was begun at Lexington in 1865, and was founded as one of the Land Grant Colleges of Agriculture and Mechanical Arts. It was founded as part of Transylvania; the university moved to its present Lexington campus in 1878. Among the specialized services of the University of Kentucky which give particular attention to the needs of the state are the Spindletop Research Center, devoted to research on new uses for coal and many other types of research; the National Tobacco Research Center; a new $8,000,000 Agricultural Research Center and a Dairy Research Center. The state's preoccupation with horses is reflected in the university's courses in equitation (riding). The University of Kentucky is now the nucleus of a statewide system of 12 public institutions of higher learning and of 28 private colleges in the state.

A landmark in higher education in the United States was the founding of Transylvania College (now university), America's oldest college west of the mountains. The college moved to Lexington and became a cultural center of note. One of its professors was Henry Clay. Another "first" in education was recorded by the University of Louisville, it is ranked as the oldest municipally owned university in the United States. Among its outstanding divisions are the Cancer Research Center, donated by the Kentucky Colonels Association; and the Potomological Institute, specializing in the study of inland waters. It is one of only three such centers in the world and the only one this side of the iron curtain.

In the Louisville area alone are eleven institutions of higher learning.

Kentucky's first school was opened in 1775 in the fort at Harrodsburg. The first public school began in 1794 at Pisgah near Lexington. Some experts say that most of Abraham Lincoln's early education came from one of the "Blab Schools," where all the pupils read their lessons at once in loud voices to show that they were studying. Needless to say, the quality of education in such schools was not high. The first statewide public school system was established in 1838. Today Kentucky ranks highest among all Southern states in the percentage of those who can read or write.

Kentucky "took a giant step ahead in education in 1966" with passage of a bill to advance to university status the four state colleges of Morehead, Eastern, Murray, and Western State. The legislature also permitted the development of a community college system.

Several fine schools have been established especially for the needs of young people in the mountain regions. Renowned around the world for this work is Pine Mountain Settlement School, founded in 1913. Henderson Settlement School near Middlesboro helped to change its region from lawlessness to peace and progress. Hindman Settlement School was the first school of this type to be set up in Kentucky.

This came about through the efforts of "Uncle Sol" Beveridge who at the age of eighty-two walked twenty miles to try to interest two women he thought might take up the work of teaching in his area. Beveridge remarked, "When I was a little chunk of a shirttailed lad, a-hoeing corn on the steep hillside, I'd get to the end of a row and look up Troublesome Creek and wonder if anybody would ever come to larn the young 'uns. Nobody ever come in. Nobody ever went out. We jist growed up and never knowed nothin. I can't read nor write; many of my chilluns can't read nor write, but I have grands and greats as is the purtiest speakin' and the easiest larnin' of any chilluns in the world. I want as they should have a chanct."

To give older people a chance to learn to read and write, Cora Wilson Stewart founded the Eastern Kentucky Moonlight Schools at Morehead in 1911, where people from eighteen to eighty-six have been taught. "One of the truly unique educational institutions of the nation" is the way Alice Lloyd Junior College at Pippa Passes has been described.

To preserve the land, educate and improve the lot of the people, such organizations as The Council of the Southern Mountains, with headquarters at Berea, and the Conservation Education Center of the Land Between the Lakes have been created.

Collecting Your Thoughts

Many things have been written about what Kentucky education will need in the future. Read more on the trends in education in the state.

Enchantment of Kentucky

People from outside Kentucky make more than 22,000,000 trips into the state each year and spend $750,000,000 in the process. The attractions are obvious—thoroughbreds and bluegrass, Mammoth Cave and natural bridges, the charm of the South combined with features of the North, beautiful mansions, pink-coated fox hunters and the revered Lincoln country.

However, there are other great lures for travelers which are not yet so well-known outside the state. Western Kentucky has become one of the largest centers of outdoor water recreation in the United States. Many experts have said that "Kentucky has the most beautiful, the finest and the most outstanding state park system in the nation." There are now forty state parks and national preserves in Kentucky. Twelve of the state parks are fully-developed luxury resorts, with some of the country's finest lodges.

Another great attraction is the Kentucky museums, particularly those that specialize in certain subjects. In another cultural field, the state has achieved one of the most unusual accomplishments ever made in serious music.

Altogether the traveler may find an unusual amount of variety and pleasure in Kentucky.

City of Louis XVI

A hush settles over 100,000 noisy people. The band plays *My Old Kentucky Home,* a tune that might seem out of place in this setting but strangely it is not; a neigh or whinny may be heard; the handsome horses paw the ground, toss their heads or quiver with anticipation; and over the hushed air sounds the strident note of a bugle shrilling forth the *Call to the Post.* Over 100,000,000 radios and television sets blast the words, "They're off!" The crowd jumps to its feet. The Run for the Roses is on once again.

Although Louisville has great industry and many cultural and entertainment attractions, almost everywhere it is most noted for "one of the two most important sporting events in the world today"—the Kentucky Derby. The Derby is the oldest race in continuous operation in the United States and was patterned after the Epsom Derby of England.

The Derby began in 1875 when park-like Churchill Downs race track was first opened. Much of the international reputation of the track and of the Derby has come about through the brilliant work of Kentucky's "Mr. Racing," Colonel Matt Winn. Today the one-mile track is a part of facilities with stalls for 1,200 horses and grandstand seats for 55,000. It has more reserved seats than any other horse racing track in the world. At the track is also a Derby Museum. It is a point of pride with Kentuckians that when 91 Derbies had been run, Kentucky horses had won 71 of them.

Before and after the Derby, on the first Saturday of May, are many festival and carnival events, including the Pegasus Parade, Queen's Coronation, Kentucky Colonels' Banquet, and a country music spectacular. As the horses rest up before their big race, another race takes place—a spectacular contest between two steamboats, the *Belle of Louisville* and the *Delta Queen* sent down the river by the Cincinnati Green Lines for the annual race. The gilded antlers of an elk is the prize for this race. In an unusual transaction the *Belle* was bought at auction by Jefferson County and now keeps the river steamboat tradition alive by carrying passengers on excursions.

The crowds and excitement of the Derby festival at Louisville are a far cry from the tiny settlement founded in 1778 by George Rogers Clark on a spit of land in the river (Corn Island), which has since been swept away. For many years the principal activity of the community was portaging cargoes around the Falls of the Ohio. In 1830 the Portland Canal was built around the falls, opening the river to traffic from Pittsburgh to the mouth of the Mississippi, and Louisville became one of the most important river ports. As early as 1799, this city had been made

a port of entry by the United States, and a hundred years later it had the only inland United States Coast Guard Station.

The city, named for King Louis XVI of France in honor of his help during the Revolution, grew rapidly. In 1831 a visitor wrote: "There are at this time about 1,200 dwelling houses in the town, mostly built of brick. Many are equal to any in the Atlantic cities. . . . There are probably more ease and affluence in this place than in any western town—their houses are splendid, substantial, and richly furnished."

Author Charles Dickens, who said many unkind things about other American cities, and some about Louisville, wrote in 1842, "We lodged as though we had been in Paris, rather than hundreds of miles beyond the Alleghanies," (sic) when he visited Louisville's Galt House.

Today, Louisville still offers to visitors many memories of its historic past. Its founder, George Rogers Clark, sleeps in Cave Hill Cemetery, itself a showplace of rare trees and shrubs. Locust Grove, the handsome Georgian mansion set on fifty acres, where Clark spent his last years, is now open to the public.

FARMINGTON

Another notable mansion is Farmington, designed by Thomas Jefferson, with an original deed signed by Patrick Henry. Here Abraham Lincoln spent some time at the invitation of his friend Joshua Fry Speed, then owner of the mansion.

Zachary Taylor and his wife are buried in Taylor National Cemetery near Louisville.

Belgravia Court and St. James Court have been restored by their private owners to show what the city was like in the past. The residents are proud of their restored fountains, gaslights and tiny gardens, recalling an opulent era of Louisville's history.

The Louisville Symphony Orchestra is one of the best known and most distinctive in the world. The orchestra has probably commissioned more works from composers than has any other and because of this, it has no doubt recorded more present-day musical works than any other orchestra. It has reached its current peak under the leadership of Conductor Roberts S. Whitney, also the Dean of the School of Music at the University of Louisville.

Two of the attractions on the university campus are the J. B. Speed Art Museum and the Rausch Planetarium. One of the seven original bronze castings of Rodin's famous statue, *The Thinker,* stands directly in front of the university's Administration Building.

The Filson Club museum has pioneer relics, Indian artifacts, coin silver works of Kentucky silversmiths, guns, items owned by such outstanding figures as Daniel Boone, George Rogers Clark, and Abraham Lincoln, and many fine library items.

Two unusual specialized museums are the Kentucky Railroad Museum and the Hillerich and Bradsby Company Museum. The railroad museum has interesting examples of the development of the American railroad, including luxurious private cars and special engines. The Hillerich and Bradsby Museum displays items reflecting the history and growth of baseball, including bats used by famous sluggers. A tour of the Hillerich and Bradsby Company demonstrates how modern bats are created.

There are many interesting museum collections at the library of Southern Baptist Theological Seminary, where there is a Billy Graham room, and one of the most complete archaeological collections of items excavated from Biblical cities. The Louisville Museum and the Art Center Association both offer other interesting displays.

The Kentucky Fair and Exposition Center provides a 375-acre complex with exposition halls, coliseum, par-three golf course and motor speedway. The exposition center is one of the world's largest multipurpose exposition buildings.

Capital City

Frankfort was founded in 1786 by James Wilkinson. He chose the name in honor of a pioneer named Frank who had been shot by the Indians. A ford in the region was already known as Frank's Ford, so the town name was easily adapted from this. In December, 1792, five commissioners chose Frankfort to be the seat of state government, a distinction it has held ever since.

It has been said that the "chief crop" of Frankfort is politics, especially when the legislature is in session in the capitol building. This building was completed in 1909 and cost nearly $2,000,000. In a general way the structure resembles the United States capitol at Washington, D. C. The interior of the dome is similar to that of Napoleon's Tomb in Paris, and the stairways have been copied from those of the Paris Opera. Incidentally, the architect spent his honeymoon in Paris.

The three-story building is surrounded by a broad stone terrace. Its outer walls are ornamented with seventy giant Ionic columns, each cut from a single block of stone. The richly sculptured north pediment shows an heroic lady, Kentucky, standing in front of a Chair of State, attended by Progress, History, Plenty, Law, Art and Labor. The rotunda floor is composed of Tennessee and Italian marble. In the rotunda are heroic statues of Kentucky's sons, Lincoln, Clay, Jefferson Davis, and Barkley. On the capitol lawn is the famed floral clock, adorned with 13,000 plants which change patterns and colors as the seasons change. A turning minute hand weighs 530 pounds.

The old statehouse building was used as a capitol from 1829 to 1910. Built in the classic Greek Revival style, it features a beautiful, self-supporting stone staircase. The building now houses the Kentucky Historical Society and its outstanding exhibits, including papers of Lincoln, Washington, Davis, Clay and others. Daniel Boone's rifle and the pistol used by Aaron Burr to kill Alexander Hamilton are featured displays.

Other public buildings include the handsome present mansion of the governor and the old mansion of governors, where the lieutenant governor now resides.

The region of the city enclosed by Wapping, Wilkinson, Washington and Main streets has been called the Corner of Celebrities. In this small area have lived nine United States senators, seven ambassadors, two justices of the United States Supreme Court, three admirals, and two U. S. Cabinet members.

Another celebrity, now at rest in the cemetery overlooking Frankfort, is Daniel Boone; the bodies of Boone and his wife were brought there from Missouri where they died. Although Boone had said he never wanted to return to Kentucky, he might have found a measure of repose and satisfaction in the honor done to him by later generations of Kentuckians.

"Aristocratic" Lexington

In 1775 an exploring party was camping on a pleasant bluegrass site when word came of the Battle of Lexington. They named the location of their camp in honor of the battle, and it has remained Lexington from that day to this. In 1779 a blockhouse was built there, and the community grew around this, made wealthy by the abundance of its agriculture, graced with "regal people and even more aristocratic horses." At one time Lexington was the most important frontier settlement of the American West.

The city has long been known as "the Athens of the West." It had the first newspaper published west of the mountains, was on the circuit of most of the traveling stage companies, had a bona fide opera house, and was so advanced in music that one of Beethoven's works received its American premiere in Lexington. Today that tradition is maintained by the Central Kentucky Philharmonic Orchestra, and by the many colleges and universities and other cultural institutions.

The University of Kentucky is particularly known for its Carnegie Museum of Anthropology, for beautiful Memorial Hall, and extensive Memorial Coliseum. Transylvania University, oldest college west of the mountains, has educated 21 college presidents, 24 distinguished military men, 32 Supreme Court justices, 57 senators, 35 state and territorial governors, 15 cabinet officers and the President of the Confederacy, Jefferson Davis. The library of Morrison College has long been known as one of the finest in the country.

ASHLAND

Near Lexington is Ashland, home of Henry Clay, and occupied by the Clay family for four generations. Hopemont was the home of dashing John Hunt Morgan. Legend says that when Morgan escaped from a federal prison he wanted to see his mother, so he rode to Lexington, dashed his horse into Hopemont, greeted his mother, and rode out through the back door to make good his escape. Hopemont was the birthplace of another family member, Thomas Hunt Morgan, winner of the Nobel Prize in 1933 for medicine and physiology.

Another home preserved at Lexington is that of Senator John Pope, who had only one arm. When a voter was asked one day why he planned to vote for Pope instead of his opponent, he answered, "He has only one arm to thrust into the treasury."

Henry Clay, John Hunt Morgan, and Vice President John C. Breckinridge are buried in the Lexington cemetery.

Lexington's greatest claim to fame, however, springs from the park-like belt of farms surrounding the city, where some of the world's most famous horses are raised. The city's preoccupation with horses is shown by the golden stallion weathervane on top of the Fayette County Courthouse. Names of many of the Lexington farms are household words. Calumet Farm was founded by W. M. Wright, who named it for the baking powder business which had brought him his fortune. Derby winners Whirlaway and Tim Tam are among the many well-known horses bearing the Calumet colors.

One of the world's best-known horses, Man o'War, died at Faraway Farm in 1947. He is buried there, and a striking statue of "Big Red" stands on a memorial at Newton Pike.

Hamburg Place was the home of six Kentucky Derby winners, and Spendthrift Farm is said to have the "most valuable aggregation of stock horses in the world." One of Spendthrift's best known was Nashua. Spindletop Farm is the location of the American Saddle Horse Museum, a collection of horse trophies, pictures and curia.

One of the best known of Kentucky horsemen was Colonel E. R. Bradley of Idle Hour Farm. He was also renowned for his kindness to employees. An employee's name was never removed from Colonel Bradley's role as long as one of the employee's dependents was living. Idle Hour Farm developed four Derby winners.

The investment and upkeep costs of the famed horse farms around Lexington are fantastic. White plank fences protect the horses who might injure themselves on wire fences, running into them because of their comparatively weak eyes. These board fences cost more than $1.00 per running foot, and the 25 miles of fencing on one farm cost more than $130,000. The four-mile field-stone fence built between Coldstream and Main Chance farms is the longest of its kind in America. No mortar was used in its construction.

One of Lexington's most popular spectator sports is horse watching. The Junior League Horse Show is the largest outdoor horse show in the country. The yearling horse auction sales at Keeneland are said to be "as glamorous as a Hollywood opening." The horses are led to the flower-bedecked salesroom and stand in the beam of spotlights for the thrilling moments of bidding. In 1964 a Bold Ruler colt brought $170,000 at the Thoroughbred Keeneland Yearling Sales.

77

Keeneland, Lexington's trotting track, holds 37 of the world's one-mile trotting and pacing records.

The Rest of Central Kentucky

The most-visited historical attractions of Kentucky are those surrounding the life of Abraham Lincoln. The "wandering" cabin where he was born was dismantled and shipped around the country on exhibition. The places it went included the Tennessee Centennial Exposition in Nashville, New York's Central Park, and the Pan-American Exposition in Buffalo. It was stored in the basement of a Long Island mansion and finally returned to Kentucky in time for the 100th anniversary of Lincoln's birth, when Theodore Roosevelt laid the cornerstone for the Lincoln Memorial near Hodgenville on February 12, 1909. This is now known as Abraham Lincoln Birthplace National Historic Site.

More than 100,000 persons contributed the funds for purchase of the cabin and farm and construction of the memorial. The cabin was taken apart and put together so many times that the dimensions were cut down one foot in width and three feet in length, due to deterioration of the log ends. The cabin is enclosed in a memorial structure fronted by six Doric columns and approached by 56 steps—one for each year of Lincoln's life. The park also includes the original spring of Thomas Lincoln's Sinking Spring farm and the huge old boundary oak. Acorns from this oak have been planted all over the nation, and its descendants are living reminders of Lincoln's Kentucky home.

On the Lincolns' Knob Creek farm is a reproduction of the birthplace cabin. The Lincoln Homestead Park near Springfield preserves the boyhood home of Lincoln's father, with a memorial to his grandfather, killed by an Indian on the site. At Harrodsburg the Lincoln Marriage Temple shelters the cabin in which the President's parents were married.

The states in which Lincoln grew and matured have established the Lincoln Heritage Trail, following the various travels of Lincoln in Illinois, Indiana, and Kentucky. The trail which led Abraham Lincoln from a humble log cabin to the White House begins in Kentucky.

RESTORATION
LINCOLN'S BOYHOOD HOME
KNOB CREEK

INDIAN BURIAL CEREMONY
MAMMOTH CAVE

Probably the next most prominent single attraction of Kentucky is a hole in the ground—but what a hole! Mammoth Cave was made a national park in 1941. One hundred and fifty miles of underground wonders have been charted. What lies beyond the explored part no one knows. Mammoth Cave is so large it holds three rivers, two lakes and one "sea." It has been used as a prehistoric burial ground and as a hall for concerts by such celebrities as violinist Ole Bull and singer Jenny Lind.

At one time patients with tuberculosis were housed in cabins in the cave in the strange hope that the damp cave air might cure them. One of the strangest facts about the cave is its "breathing." The temperature of the cave remains at 54° the year round. When the outside temperature is above that, the cave breathes out; when the outside temperature drops, the cave breathes in.

Kentucky's "Cave Country" contains many other interesting caverns such as Hidden River Cave under the town of Horse Cave and nearby Mammoth Onyx Cave.

Another popular Kentucky attraction is the stately house named Federal Hill at Bardstown, which was probably the inspiration for Foster's *My Old Kentucky Home*. A song and dance drama, *The Stephen Foster Story,* is now produced every year at Bardstown. Beginning in 1934, Stephen Collins Foster Memorial Day has been celebrated in Kentucky every year on January 31. This is the date of the original copyright for *My Old Kentucky Home.*

Bardstown's St. Joseph's Proto-Cathedral has a collection of paintings given by the king of France and valued at a million dollars. Near Bardstown is Abbey of Our Lady of Gethsemane, first Trappist monastery in the country. In contrast to this is the nearby Barton Museum of Whiskey History.

Bowling Green takes its unusual name from the fact that lawyers who came to county court used to pass their idle time bowling on the green of Robert Moore's home. Today Bowling Green is the home of Western Kentucky University. The Kentucky Building houses a particularly fine museum of state subjects and an outstanding collection of Kentucky writing.

One of the state's finest natural attractions is Cumberland Falls, over which tumbles the largest volume of water of any falls east of the Rockies, except Niagara. At night, when conditions are right, the spectacle of the "moonbow" may be seen. Only one other falls in the western hemisphere has a moonbow. The Cumberland Falls State Park came about through donation of the land by T. Coleman du Pont.

Picturesque Danville was Kentucky's first capital. Centre College here gained unusual fame in 1920 when it had a football team (the Praying Colonels), which defeated some of the country's greatest teams. Near Danville is the Pioneer Playhouse, the official "State Theatre" of Kentucky, the only theater in the nation devoted entirely to presentation of new plays.

America's largest colony of Shakers was established at Pleasant Hill near Harrodsburg. This community is now being restored at a cost of $2,000,000, with an arts and crafts center, a residential center for educational seminars, and an exhibition center of life of the Shakers. Old Fort Harrod State Park features a reproduction of the fort.

A more prominent fort in today's news is Fort Knox, where America's pure gold, worth more than $12,000,000,000, is stored in the Gold Bullion Depository. The 20-ton vault door can only be opened by the combined efforts of several people, each of whom knows only a part of the combination. As an army base, the fort is headquarters for mechanized operations, and the Patton Museum has a fascinating display of historic armored equipment.

Covington has been described as being "like a city on the Rhine." It is especially known for its Behringer Museum of Natural History. Its Monte Casino Chapel is known as the world's smallest church, seating only one person. Adjoining Newport has come a long way since its river banks were stained with blood of duelists.

Near Paris, Claibourne Farm has produced some of the world's great horses, including Gallant Fox winner of the 1930 Kentucky Derby. The denomination known as the Christian Church had its beginning at Paris, springing from a meeting of twenty to thirty thousand people at the Cane Ridge Meeting House. This meeting has been called "the most remarkable religious assemblage ever known on the continent."

Nicholasville is known for its Animal Forest Zoo, where many of the animals roam free. Its collection of exotic birds is one of the finest in the country.

There is much of interest for the visitor on the Berea College campus at Berea. Boone Tavern, owned by the college, is one of the country's finest eating places. Most of the beautiful hand-rubbed furniture of the Boone Tavern dining room and hotel has been made by students. They also operate a candy kitchen, print shop, needlework and craft shops, and a dairy farm as well as the hotel. The Berea College Country Dancers are well known. The college art department gallaries exhibit student work. The store of the Churchill Weavers displays interesting hand products, and there is also a museum in the building.

Western Kentucky

The metropolis of western Kentucky is Paducah, where the Tennessee River meets the Ohio, surveyed and plotted in 1827 by William Clark, of Lewis and Clark fame. He named the town for his Indian friend Paduke. The city has painted a red line along its streets to guide the visitor to 51 noteworthy sights. Statues and monuments include those of Paduke and native sons Irvin S. Cobb and Alben W. Barkley. Wickliffe, near Paducah, is said to be the nation's number one museum of excavated relics of the prehistoric Mound Builders. One of Paducah's notable buildings is the city hall, designed by famed architect Edward Durell Stone.

Columbus was laid out with the expectation that it would be chosen as capital of the United States. Clinton remembers its famous son, Casey Jones, with a monument. A unique monument was created at Maplewood Cemetery, Mayfield, by horsetrader Henry Wooldridge. He had 16 life-sized statues made depicting assorted relatives and friends, and had himself included twice, all facing east. Fulton is known for its banana festival in late September, when visitors receive free bananas.

Another festival is Benton's Big Singing, held the fourth Sunday in May; large crowds assemble to sing from William Walker's Southern Harmony songbook. The singers sing from shaped notes in a style handed down from generation to generation.

Kentucky's Land Between the Lakes region is being developed as the pilot for similar future national recreation areas. More than 600,000 visitors enjoyed the region in 1965. One attraction is Kentucky Lake's Fishing Derby with $5,000 in prizes.

Ten miles from Hopkinsville is Fairview. At this birthplace of Jefferson Davis, a 351-foot monument in his memory, very much like the Washington Monument in the nation's capital, has been erected. This is said to be the tallest cast concrete obelisk ever built. Public subscription raised $200,000 for the monument, which was dedicated in 1924. Also at Davis State Park is a replica of the log birthplace of the Confederate president, one of the few such cabins that had windows.

The Shaker Museum at Auburn contains furniture and utensils used and often originated by members of the Shaker cult, more formally known as the United Society of Believers in Christ's Second Appearance. They were given their nickname of Shakers from the peculiar swaying prayer dance.

Logan County is proud of its remarkable record of producing five United States senators, four governors of Kentucky and five governors of other states.

Russellville still remembers its moment of terror when Jesse James began his criminal career in 1868 by robbing the Russellville bank. Another "crime" was committed at Adairville, when Andrew Jackson, one day to become President, killed Charles Dickinson in a duel and almost wrecked his own promising career.

Cloverport is the site where the Lincoln family crossed the Ohio River on their way from Kentucky to Indiana.

One of Kentucky's most interesting state parks is Audubon. Here are two lakes described in Audubon's writings in which he told of the many migratory birds that still flock there. The John James Audubon Memorial Museum has many original Audubon paintings, the finest Kentucky collection of his prints, and other exhibits of Audubon's stay in the Henderson region. Nesting holes in the tower of the building welcome the birds Audubon loved so well.

On the campus of Murray State University in Murray, stands a monument to remind the world that the true inventor of radio is often considered to be Nathan B. Stubblefield, a semi-recluse who lived in a cabin just off the university campus.

Eastern Kentucky

Ashland takes its name from Henry Clay's home in Lexington. It is a steel-making center and industrial hub of the eastern border. A notable event is the American Folk Song Festival, founded by Jean Thomas, and held each June on the grounds of the founder's Wee House in the Wood. A rough stage is built in front of a century old McGuffey log schoolhouse. Courting and answer-back ballads, work songs of the Big Sandy, and topical songs which were popular when the early settlers were arriving—all are kept alive here. Accompaniment is provided by cornstalk fiddles, gourd banjos and dulcimers. Miss Thomas' museum-home is open to visitors the year round.

There is a tradition that George Washington once owned land at Louisa. The unique Fort Gay bridge there crosses two rivers, connects two states, two counties and two towns. Blue Licks Battlefield State Park is near Olivet. Another state park is Natural Bridge, near Slade. The 65-foot bridge that gives the park its name is only one of several of these interesting natural features to be found in Kentucky.

Near London is another state park, Levi Jackson, with its interesting Mountain Life Museum. McHargue's Mill at London shows one of the world's largest collections of millstones. Breaks Interstate Park preserves the natural beauty of a spectacular gorge between Kentucky and Virginia.

The Daniel Boone festival at Barbourville is one of the country's most unusual. Here is held each year the old fashioned long rifle shooting contest between Kentucky and Pennsylvania. There is constant rivalry over the name of the long rifle, whether it should be called the Kentucky rifle or the Pennsylvania rifle. Whichever state wins the contest has the right to name the rifle in its honor for the coming year. At the festival also are square dances, musket shooting, a pageant—the signing of the Cherokee Cane Treaty—and old time fiddling. Reproduced near Barbourville in Dr. Thomas Walker State Park is the doctor's cabin, the first one in Kentucky.

Pine Mountain State Park near Pineville has the outstanding Mountain Laurel Festival. Highlight of the festival is the crowning of the Mountain Laurel Queen, chosen from the most beautiful girls at Kentucky's colleges. Also given each summer in the park is the Biblical pageant "The Book of Job." Sweeping across the great Pine Mountain region is the Little Shepherd Trail, named in honor of the *Little Shepherd* book.

An unusual community celebration is Harlan's Poke Sallet Festival during the last week in June. Poke, a tender, green herb native to the area, is picked in the spring at the peak of perfection and carefully frozen for the main feast. The menu consists of poke cooked with slabs of streaked sow belly and served with "biled" eggs, garden-fresh green onions, cornbread, and ice-cold buttermilk. The official "Poke Warden" is traditionally the governor of the Commonwealth of Kentucky.

Although many of the mountain customs are disappearing, the visitor may still find traces of interesting mountain ways and innumerable stories and legends about the mountain life. Such picturesque place names as Lonesome, Red Fox, Pumpkin Center, Peevish, Troublesome Creek, Hell-Fer-Sartain, Polecat Creek and Cut Shin Creek show the independence and imagination of the mountain people.

The mountain people continue to be proud and independent as well as generous and hospitable. In spite of the hard life, many of them are able and willing to follow the last part of the advice once given to a bride on how to do the wash by hand. The advice closed with the words, "go put on cleen dress, smooth hair with side combs, brew cup of tee, set and rest and rock a spell and count blessins."

The place where the entire great western movement in America started is now preserved as Cumberland Gap National Historic Park. The startling break in the Cumberlands where Tennessee, Virginia and Kentucky meet, was named in honor of the Duke of Cumberland.

When Henry Clay stood at Cumberland Gap, he was not thinking only of the struggling pioneers of the past, but as he said prophetically, "I am listening to the tread of the coming millions." The millions have arrived in Kentucky to live there, to enjoy its beauty, and to use its resources wisely. Clay's forecast has come true.

CUMBERLAND GAP

Handy Reference Section

Instant Facts

Became the 15th state, June 1, 1792
Capital—Frankfort, founded 1786
State Motto—United We Stand, Divided We Fall
Familiar Name—Bluegrass State
State Bird—Cardinal
State Fish—Bass
State Tree—Tulip Poplar
State Flower—Goldenrod
State Song—*My Old Kentucky Home,* by Stephen Collins Foster
Area—40,395 square miles
Greatest Length (north to south)—175 miles
Greatest Width (east to west)—350 miles
Highest Point—4,150 feet (Big Black Mountain, Harlan County)
Lowest Point—257 feet (Fulton County at Mississippi River)
Geographic Center—Marlon (near Lebanon)
Highest Recorded Temperature—114° (Greensburg)
Lowest Recorded Temperature—minus 34° (Bonnieville and Cynthiana)
Population—3,179,000 (1965 estimate)
Population Density—76.2 persons per square mile (1960 census)

Principal Cities—		
Louisville	389,000	(1960 census)
Lexington	62,810	
Covington	60,376	
Owensboro	42,471	
Paducah	34,479	
Ashland	31,283	
Newport	30,070	

You Have a Date with History

1654—Colonel Wood explores Kentucky
1673—Arthur and Needham explore in general area
1739—M. Longueil discovers Big Bone Lick
1750—Celeron, Sieur de Bienville, claims region for France
1751—Christopher Gist explores
1756—French traders establish village opposite Portsmouth, Ohio
1763—George III prohibits settlement
1769—Daniel Boone first visits Kentucky
1774—Harrodsburg becomes first permanent European settlement
1775—Boonsborough begun

1776—Kentucky organized as a Virginia county
1777—Indian attacks leave Kentucky almost desolate
1778—Louisville founded
1779—Lexington founded
1782—British driven from Kentucky
1785—Danville made seat of Kentucky government
1792—Statehood and first constitution
1799—Mammoth Cave discovered
1809—Abraham Lincoln born near Hodgenville
1811—Strong earthquakes; first steamboat
1818—Jackson Purchase adds western Kentucky
1832—First railroad operates in Kentucky
1860—Kentucky voters reject Lincoln and Breckinridge
1861—Kentucky "neutrality" recognized
1862—Battle of Perryville
1866—First bridge across Ohio River
1875—First Kentucky Derby
1892—N. B. Stubblefield transmits voice by wireless
1900—Governor William Goebel shot
1917—World War I begins, in which 75,043 from Kentucky served
1924—First state park established
1936—State government reorganized
1937—Worst Ohio River flood in history
1941—World War II begins, during which 323,798 from Kentucky served
1962—Kentucky wins "Keep America Beautiful" award
1965—Kentucky celebrates three billionth ton of coal mined in the Commonwealth

89

Thinkers, Doers, Fighters

People of renown who have been associated with Kentucky

Audubon, John James
Barkley, Alben
Beard, Dan Carter
Bibb, John B.
Boone, Daniel
Breckinridge, John C.
Burnside, Ambrose E.
Clark, George Rogers
Clay, Henry
Cobb, Irvin S.
Davis, Jefferson
Fitch, John
Fox, John, Jr.
Griffith, David Wark
Guthrie, A. B.
Harlan, John M.
Hood, John B.
Johnson, Richard M.
Johnston, Albert Sidney

Kelly, William
Lawton, Henry W.
Lincoln, Abraham
McAdam, John
McDowell, Ephraim
Morgan, John Hunt
Niles, John Jacob
Rice, Alice Hegan
Stevenson, Adlai E., I
Stuart, Jesse
Stubblefield, Nathan
Taylor, Zachary
Thomas, Jean
Vinson, Fred M.
Warren, Robert Penn
Whitney, Mrs. C. V.
Winn, Matt
Woodfill, Samuel

Annual Events

April—Lions Club Minstrels, Paris
April—Tater Day, Benton
April-May—Kentucky Derby Festival, Louisville
May—Mountain Laurel Festival, Pineville
May—Governor's Cup Regatta, Kenlake State Park
May—Open House, Louisville
May—Horse Show, Pikeville
May—National Coon Hunters Meeting and Hunt, Paducah
May—Big Singing, Benton
May—Strawberry Festivals, Adairville and Greenville
May-June—Jessamine County Horse Show, Nicholasville
June—Poke Sallet Festival
June—American Folk Song Festival, Ashland
June—Wickliffe Horse Show, Wickliffe
July—Shaker Festival, Auburn
July—Blackberry Festival, Carlisle
August—Horse Show, Pikeville
July—Junior League Horse Show, Lexington

September—State Fair and Horse Show, Louisville
September-October—International Banana Festival, Fulton
October—Cherokee Cane Treaty, Pine Mountain State Park
October—Daniel Boone Festival, Barbourville
October—Tobacco Festivals, Russellville and Carrollton
October—Court Day, Mount Sterling
November—Blessing of the Hounds, Lexington
November—Lions Club Minstrels, Fulton
Other annual horse shows—Lawrenceburg, Lexington, Paris, Burkesville,
Cynthiana, Frankfort, Lancaster, Georgetown, Greensburg, Munfordville,
New Castle, Nicholasville, Richmond, Harrodsburg, Jamestown,
Shelbyville, Campbellsville, Versailles

Governors of the State of Kentucky

Isaac Shelby, 1792–1796
James Garrard, 1796–1804
Christopher Greenup, 1804–1808
Charles Scott, 1808–1812
Isaac Shelby, 1812–1816
George Madison, 1816
Gabriel Slaughter, 1816–1820
John Adair, 1820–1824
Joseph Desha, 1824–1828
Thomas Metcalfe, 1828–1832
John Breathitt, 1832–1834
James T. Morehead, 1834–1836
James Clark, 1836–1839
Charles A. Wickliffe, 1839–1840
Robert P. Letcher, 1840–1844
William Owsley, 1844–1848
John J. Crittenden, 1848–1850
John L. Helm, 1850–1851
Lazarus W. Powell, 1851–1855
Charles S. Morehead, 1855–1859
Beriah Magoffin, 1859–1862
James F. Robinson, 1862–1863
Thomas E. Bramlette, 1863–1867
John L. Helm, 1867
John W. Stevenson, 1867–1871
Preston H. Leslie, 1871–1875

James B. McCreary, 1875–1879
Luke P. Blackburn, 1879–1883
J. Proctor Knott, 1883–1887
Simon Bolivar Buckner, 1887–1891
John Young Brown, 1891–1895
William O. Bradley, 1895–1899
William S. Taylor, 1899–1900
William Goebel, 1900
J. C. W. Beckham, 1900–1907
Augustus E. Willson, 1907–1911
James B. McCreary, 1911–1915
Augustus O. Stanley, 1915–1919
James D. Black, 1919
Edwin P. Morrow, 1919–1923
William J. Fields, 1923–1927
Flem D. Sampson, 1927–1931
Ruby Laffoon, 1931–1935
Albert B. Chandler, 1935–1939
Keen Johnson, 1939–1943
Simeon S. Willis, 1943–1947
Earle C. Clements, 1947–1950
Lawrence W. Wetherby, 1950–1955
Albert B. Chandler, 1955–1959
Bert T. Combs, 1959–1963
Edward T. Breathitt, 1963–

INDEX

About the Author: Allan Carpenter was born in Waterloo, Iowa. He went to Iowa State College and then taught at a Des Moines Junior High School and at Drake University. He left teaching to found the magazine *Teachers Digest* which he published for eight years. He has been associated with publishing for many years and now works full time as a free-lance writer. His first book was published when he was twenty and since then he has written over fifty books.

About the Artist: Darrell Wiskur lives in Aurora, Illinois, with his wife and two small sons. He is a free-lance artist who spends most of his time illustrating books for children. He had his formal art training at the Chicago Academy of Fine Art and at the School of Professional Art. He enjoys hunting and fishing, and his love of nature and the out-of-doors is reflected in his work.